PREFACE

This book Life-changing Thoughts on Prayer Vol. 5 is the eighteenth in the *Prayer Power series*. The books in this series that have already been written are:

1. The Way Of Victorious Praying
2. The Ministry Of Fasting
3. The Art Of Intercession
4. The Practice Of Intercession
5. Praying With Power
6. Practical Spiritual Warfare Through Prayer
7. Moving God Through Prayer
8. The Ministry Of Praise And Thanksgiving
9. Waiting On The Lord In Prayer
10. The Ministry Of Supplication
11. Life-Changing Thoughts On Prayer (Vol. 1)
12. The Centrality of Prayer
13. Life-Changing Thoughts On Prayer (Vol. 2)
14. Prayer and Spiritual Intimacy
15. Life-Changing Thoughts on Prayer (Vol. 3)
16. The Art of Worship

17. Life-Changing Thoughts on Prayer (Vol. 4)
18. Life-Changing Thoughts on Prayer (Vol. 5)
19. Learning to Importune in Prayer
20. Prayer And A Walk With God
21. From His Prayer files
22. Prayer and Holiness
23. Practical Helps in Fasting Long Fasts
24. Life-Changing Thoughts on Fasting (Vol 1)
25. Life-Changing Thoughts on Fasting (Vol 2)

Prayer is central to any work and to any move of God. We have been burdened for very many years about praying, and are labouring to pray ever-increasingly. We have been burdened about the centrality of prayer and have laboured to lead individuals into seeing the necessity of prayer, and to actually pray. We have been burdened to lead churches into seeing the necessity of prayer and into praying. As I prayed alone, as I led others in prayer and as we travelled and taught on prayer, I took down key thoughts for myself that came through. In this book, we share with you some of the thoughts that came through between 3 July 2005 and 3 February 2009. Our prayer is that by God's grace you would find in this book some thoughts that will stir your heart to pray and pray and pray and revolutionalise your prayer life. May our God bless you exceedingly.

Your brother in Christ,

Zacharias Tanee Fomum
P.O BOX 6090
Yaounde - Cameroon

LIFE-CHANGING THOUGHTS ON PRAYER

Volume 5

PRAYER POWER SERIES
BOOK 18

ZACHARIAS TANEE FOMUM

Copyright © 2009 by Zacharias Tanee Fomum
All rights reserved.

No part of this book may be reproduced in any form or by any electronic or mechanical means, including information storage and retrieval systems, without written permission from the author, except for the use of brief quotations in a book review.

Published by

A division of the Book Ministry of Christian Missionary Fellowship International

info@books4revival.com

1
PRAYER AND HOLINESS

The prayer that builds the praying person the most is the praying that is done alone. Alone before God, the praying person faces his heart in utter truth and as he waits before God in prayer, light from heaven dawns on his heart revealing his heart to him as God sees it. As this light shines on the heart, the praying one sees things as God sees them and so uproots those things in the heart that should not be there. The person then leaves the place of prayer having made spiritual progress by removing what God does not want.

Yaounde, 03/07/05
First Prayer Crusade for Revival Worldwide

2
PRAYER AND HOLINESS

The prayer that builds up the praying person the most is the praying done alone. During prayer alone, the praying one sees his heart as God sees it and so sees the things that are needed for their heart to be like that of the Lord; and as the things are seen, they are prayed through. As a result, God enriches the heart of the praying one, and he leaves the place of prayer having made progress by growth in having more and more of what God wants on his heart.

Yaounde, 03/07/05,
First Prayer Crusade for Revival Worldwide

3
SUBMISSION

Submission is an attitude of heart which says that the will of the Lord Jesus Christ and His will alone be done on earth. The submissive one sets out to overthrow every will that operates on earth that is not the will of the Lord Jesus Christ. The submissive one will wield the mighty weapons of fasting and prayer to ensure that all wills that are rebellious to the will of the Lord Jesus Christ's are demolished without mercy. Submission is an attitude of ruthless warfare against all that has its origin in the mind of the wicked one.

Yaounde, 03/07/05,
First Prayer Crusade for Revival Worldwide

PRAYER

The Holy Spirit presides over all prayer meetings regardless of which of His children is used to lead the meeting at the human level.

So, true believers take every prayer meeting seriously regardless of which of God's children is being used to lead the prayer meeting.

Yaounde, 04/07/05
First Fast for Revival in Christian Missionary Fellowship International
First Fast against the Host of Hinduism, Buddhism and Islam worldwide

5
PRAYER AND HOLINESS

The Holy Spirit presides over all prayer meetings. He comes to pray in those whose hearts are pure and to pray through those whose hearts are pure.

Because of His holiness, the Holy Spirit cannot pray in the heart or through the heart of the one who deliberately hides a sin in his heart.

Yaounde, 04/07/05
First Fast for Revival in Christian Missionary Fellowship International
First Fast against the Host of Hinduism, Buddhism and Islam worldwide

PRAYER

The Lord prayed from the age of 12 years for a period of 18 years for 3.5 years of ministry. After 3.5 years of ministry, He had already invested (2005 − 34)[1] years into prayer so that the work of 3.5 years should bear fruit.

18 years for 3.5 years of ministry followed by 1971 years of intercession for impact.

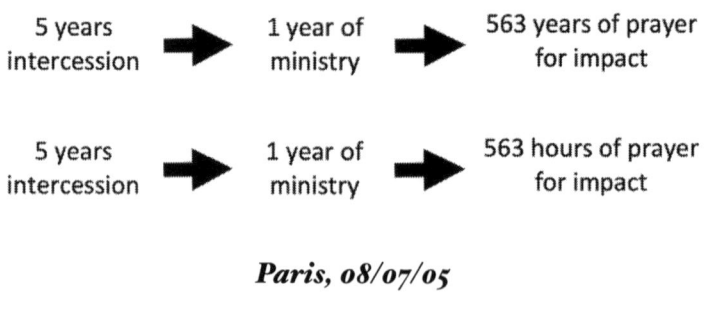

Paris, 08/07/05

---

1. Present year − 34 years, will give us the number of years already invested in prayer by the Lord Jesus, since the above text was written in 2005 not the present date.

PRAYER

Preaching that does not flow from prayer and preaching that is not followed by prayer is falsehood; it is hypocrisy.

Paris, 08/07/05

8
LEADERSHIP AND PRAYER

*L*eadership is the call to wait at the place of prayer until what is on the heart of God is imparted to the heart of the leader, so that the leader has on his heart what God has on His heart. The leader then becomes God's co-worker. The leader and God then have the same burden as concerns what God has in mind for that leadership.

Yamoussoukro, 06/08/05,
First Crusade for Personal Holiness,
Second Prayer Crusade for Personal Revival, 10th
Ivorian Convention

9
LEADERSHIP AND PRAYER

*L*eadership is the call to spend time, much time, protracted periods in God's presence so that the Lord may reveal to the leader, the heavenly model of what he is to build on earth for the Lord. Until leadership has seen clearly the heavenly model of what God has in mind to do, all activities called serving the Lord are works of the flesh and can only produce wood, hay and stubble.

Yamoussoukro, 06/08/05,
First Crusade for Personal Holiness,
Second Prayer Crusade for Personal Revival, 10th Ivorian Convention

PRAYER

We do not pray according to the imaginations of our heads. We pray according to the revelations of the Lord. **Prayer begins in the heart of God.** He reveals what is in His heart to a person. That person then knows what God will do. He then prays that God would do what God has revealed would be on His heart. He continues to pray until God answers. When prayer has thus been answered, it is the establishment on earth of that which originates in the heart of God.

Rome, 07/09/05,
Prayer Crusade for Personal Holiness, 2nd Prayer Crusade

PRAYER

The God of heaven is utterly rich and the riches in heaven so immense that He seeks real "askers". The Lord said to me, "The storehouse of heaven is still so full. All the major packets are there and all the really big ones. There is no one to ask for them. There is no one to receive them. My children are caught up with asking for trifles and true substances are not attended to. Oh that some would arise and seek great things for My glory and ask accordingly!"

Rome, 07/09/05,
First Crusade for Personal Holiness,
2nd Prayer Crusade for Revival Worldwide

12
PRAYER

*S*elf stands in the way of prayer than any other thing in creation. It is a master enemy.

Lord, deliver me from the burdens created by my self that was hurt.

Lord, deliver me from the burdens created by the fact that someone else was more successful than I.

Lord, deliver me from burdens created by the fact that someone else received more honour, praise and exaltation than I.

Lord, deliver me from the burdens created by the fact that someone outclassed me.

Lord, deliver me from burdens created by the fact that praise for what I did was given to another.

Rome, 07/09/05,
First Crusade for Personal Holiness,
2nd Prayer Crusade for Revival Worldwide

13
PRAYER

When what God wants to do is revealed to a person, that person becomes the custodian of what God wants to do. Such a person will take no rest and give God no rest until God does what he has revealed He wants to do. Such a person will pray, fast, obey, act, ... radically, totally, increasingly, until God is moved to bring to pass His will that He has revealed.

Rome, 07/09/05,
First Crusade for Personal Holiness,
2nd Prayer Crusade for Personal Revival

14
PRAYING FOR RESULTS

I commit myself not to pray in order to count the hours of prayers. I will pray to be heard. I will specialize in the type of prayer requests that God will not incidentally answer, but in those that God will have to go out of His way to answer. I will write 520 prayer requests of the kind that only God can answer and pray them through.

Kampala, 25/11/05,
2nd Prayer Crusade for Revival Worldwide,
The fifty-two-day fast

15

PRAYING AND HOLINESS

The first thing of importance is not to pray. The first thing is to qualify to pray. A person qualifies to pray by having a sin-free heart so that God will hear his prayers unceasingly. The Lord Jesus said,

> ... *"Father, I thank you that you have heard me. I knew that you always hear me, but I said this for the benefit of the people standing here, that they may believe that you sent me"* (John 11:41–42).

I must become a man whom God Almighty will always hear and answer!!!

I must be spotlessly pure twenty-four hours a day. I must dwell in the perfect holiness of God unceasingly. My desires must radiate the holiness of God. My

- motives,
- thoughts,
- looks,
- gazes,

- attitudes,
- dispositions,
- tastes,
- values,
- words,
- deeds and
- possessions must radiate the holiness of God.

I commit myself to the perfection of God, to the highest level that is possible on earth for one redeemed by the grace of God.

I must pray and be heard by God always, unceasingly!!!

__Kampala, 25/11/05,__
__2nd Prayer Crusade for Revival Worldwide,__
__The fifty-two-day fast__

16
PRAYER

When a person enters into God's presence to pray, he is like the high priest who enters the Holy of holies. How can anyone carry sin into His holy presence? What would have been the high priest's lot had he carried sin into the Holy of holies? The believer in the new covenant also comes into God's presence in prayer with fear and trembling out of a holy fear of the God of heaven, who has become his Father through the death and resurrection of the Lord Jesus.

Maputo, 28/11/05,
2nd Prayer Crusade for Revival Worldwide,
The fifty-two-day fast

17
PRAYING AND HOLINESS

*P*rayer is a life and not just an activity. Whether a person will be heard by God will depend on the person's relationship with God before he starts praying, while praying, and after praying. The person who wants to be heard by the God of holiness must be holy before prayer, holy during prayer and holy after prayer.

Maputo, 28/11/05,
2nd Prayer Crusade for Revival Worldwide,
THE FIFTY-TWO-DAY FAST

18
PRAYER AND THE WILL OF THE LORD

Regardless of a person's degree of sanctification and power to pray, God will only answer prayer that is in the will of God. Intensive praying, pleading and fasting that is not in the perfect will of God will be done in vain. God will not answer. The holiness of God and the man of holiness know that anything apart from the will of God is great evil. Consequently, no one dares even think that something that is not the will of God should be prayed. To pray that which is not the will of God is to desire that the will of Satan should be done because all that is not the will of God is the will of Satan.

I commit myself exclusively to that which is the will of God. I commit myself to ascertain that something is of the will of God before I start to pray about it. Only that which is in the will of God can be carried by the Holy Spirit to heaven, the holy dwelling place of God.

Maputo, 28/11/05,

*2nd Prayer Crusade for Revival Worldwide,
The fifty-two-day fast*

19
PRAYER AND HOLINESS

True prayer is dealing with the God of heaven. For prayer to be answered, it must be heard by the God of heaven who dwells in heaven, His holy dwelling place. The prayer must flow from a Holy heart. The prayer of an unholy person cannot reach God's dwelling place, and consequently, can never be answered. For prayer to get to heaven, God's dwelling place, the Holy Spirit must carry it there, for unless He does it, there is no way that the words of man can ever get to heaven. The prayers that flow from an impure heart cannot be touched by the Holy Spirit because His holiness makes this impossible for Him and the sinner to be united in the ministry of prayer. So, it is a settled matter that the one who knowingly allow any sin in his heart has decided that his prayers should not be heard, and they will not be heard.

Maputo, 28/11/05,
2nd Prayer Crusade for Revival Worldwide,
The fifty-two-day fast

20
LEADERSHIP AND PRAYER

Following a leader is following him to the place of his praying. This is central. This is determinant. Those who believe him pray with him and pray for him. If he prays increasingly, his leadership will grow increasingly. If he prays ever so increasingly, his leadership will grow ever so increasingly.

Yaounde, 05/12/05,
2nd Prayer Crusade for Revival Worldwide,
The fifty-two-day fast

21
LEADERSHIP AND PRAYER

A spiritual leader is a man of prayer. If his priority is not praying, he has put God aside; he has derailed. He has moved from the spiritual to the natural if prayer alone has not been centralized and prayer with others made a close second.

Yaounde, 05/12/05,
2nd Prayer Crusade for Revival Worldwid,
The fifty-two-day fast

22

CONCLUDING THE FIFTY-TWO-DAY FAST

*T*he person who has not moved God to act in a given situation has not prayed.

Dakar, 17/12/05,
Concluding the 2nd Prayer Crusade for Revival Worldwide,
The fifty-two-day fast

23

CONCLUDING THE FIFTY-TWO-DAY FAST

*P*rayer is moving God to act in a specific situation.

***Dakar, 17/12/05,
2nd Prayer Crusade for Revival Worldwide,
The fifty-two-day fast***

24
PRAYER

*A*ll that does not flow from prayer is rebellion. The rebel has decided that he can do things without God intervening in answer to prayer.

Yaounde, 25/01/06,
3rd Prayer Crusade for Revival Worldwide,
The 2nd fifty-two-day fast

25
PRAYER

All that does not flow from prayer is wood, hay and stubble. All that does not flow from prayer is a work of the flesh and Judgement Day will expose it for what it is indeed, even if it is applauded today.

Yaounde, 25/01/06,
3rd Prayer Crusade for Revival Worldwide,
The 2nd fifty-two-day fast

26

CONCLUDING THE SECOND FIFTY-TWO-DAY FAST

The reason many men do not accept Jesus as their Saviour is because they are held by demons. Each unbeliever must be liberated from that which holds sway over him so that he can believe in the Lord Jesus Christ unto eternal life.

Lome, 29/01/06,
3rd Prayer Crusade for Revival Worldwide,
The 2nd fifty-two-day fast

27

CONCLUDING THE SECOND FIFTY-TWO-DAY FAST

FASTING AND PRAYER FOR THE WINNING OF THE LOST

A reason why there are so few people saved is that there are so few people who fast and pray that captives held by Satan be released. When the saints fast and pray, the power of Satan is weakened and his captives can be released to believe the gospel. Without this work against the devil, victory in the winning of the lost will be slow.

Lome, 29/01/06,
3rd Prayer Crusade for Revival Worldwide,
The 2nd fifty-two-day fast

28
PRAYER AND HOLINESS

The power of a person's prayer is directly proportional to the holiness of his life. If a person is holy, his life will be powerful. If his prayers are powerful, they will reach heaven, God's holy dwelling place, and bring answers from the God of holiness.

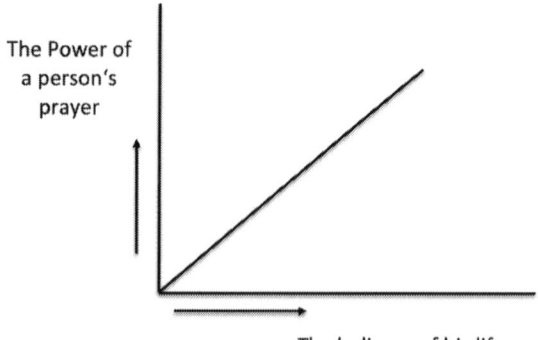

Lome, 30/01/06,
3rd Prayer Crusade for Revival Worldwide,
The 2nd fifty-two-day fast

29
PRAYER AND HOLINESS

The power of a man's prayer life is directly proportional to the man's hatred for sin. Prayers are weakened by sin in the life of the praying man. When the life is sin-free, his prayers are carried by the Holy Spirit to the throne of God. When the life is filled with sin, prayer is nearly impossible.

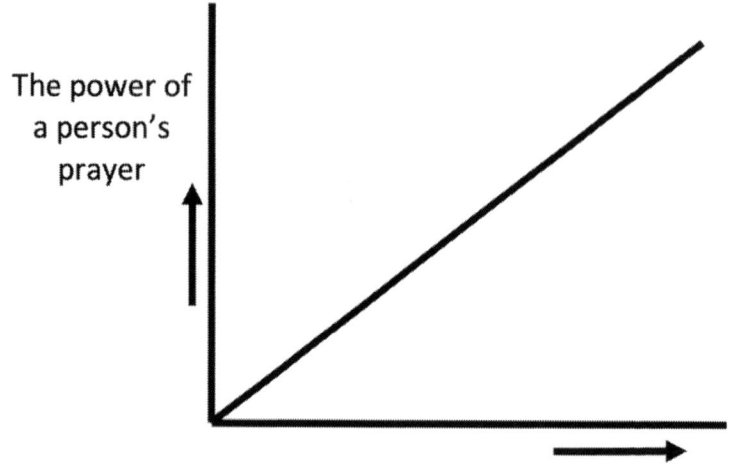

Lome, 30/01/06,
3rd Prayer Crusade for Revival Worldwide,
The 2nd fifty-two-day fast

30
APPROACHING THE ALMIGHTY

*B*efore seeking to approach the Most High, we need to "prepare" our hearts.

> *Yet if you devote your heart to him and stretch out your hands to him, if you put away the sin that is in your hand and allow no evil to dwell in your tent, then you will lift up your face without shame, you will stand firm and without fear* (Job 11:13–15).

- Standing firm before the Lord without fear
- Standing firm before God
- Face lifted up without shame to the
- Face lifted up to the Lord
- No evil allowed in the heart
- Sin in the hand put away
- Hands stretched
- Heart devoted to God

Yaounde, 13/02/06,
3rd Prayer Crusade for Revival Worldwide,
The 2nd fifty-two-day fast

APPROACHING THE ALMIGHTY PRAYER AND HOLINESS

I commit myself never to intercede for anyone or for any situation until I have waited before God and received the testimony that all is right between God and me. I refuse to utter in prayer words that will not reach the throne of the Almighty.

Yaounde, 13/02/06,
3rd Prayer Crusade for Revival Worldwide,
The 2nd fifty-two-day fast

32
PRAYER

Prayer is a longing, not so much for what God can give but for God Himself.

Yaounde, 27/02/06,
3rd Prayer Crusade for Revival Worldwide,
The 2nd fifty-two-day fast

33
PRAYER

*I*n prayer a man and God come into union and as the union and communion continue, the life of God flows into the man. If he prays for a short period, a little of God flows into him. If he prays for a longer period, more of God flows into him. How much of God a person has, depends upon how much time God and the person spend in secret union. Yes, the secret union between God and man allows God to give Himself to man. It is not surprising that the Lord Jesus Christ said,

> *But when you pray, go into your room, close the door and pray to your Father, who is unseen. Then your Father, who sees what is done in secret, will reward you* (Mathew 6:6).

**Yaounde, 27/02/06,
3rd Prayer Crusade for Revival Worldwide,
The 2nd fifty-two-day fast**

34
PRAYER AND BEING

When I pray, what flows to God is not my words or my acts. What flows to God is my being. In prayer, my being flows to God.

> *Libreville, 06/03/06*
> *The 2nd fifty-two-day fast*

35
PRAYER AND A MAN'S BEING

When a man prays, his being and his words are carried into God's presence. If his being and his words are one, the Lord receives the prayer and He answers. If the being and the words are not one, the prayer is rejected. God cannot answer a hypocrite; for a hypocrite is one whose heart and words are not one, or whose words and being are not one.

Libreville, 06/03/06,
The 2nd fifty-two-day fast

36
PRAYER

The central thing in prayer is asking and receiving from the Almighty.

Lilongwe, 15/03/06,
The 2nd fifty-two-day fast

37
PRAYER

The goal of prayer is not to draw the attention of people to the praying person, but to draw the attention of God to the praying person and prayer request.

Lilongwe, 15/03/06,
The 2nd fifty-two-day fast

38
PRAYER AND THE SPIRIT-FILLED CHURCH

When the entire church perseveres in one place of prayer constantly, the Holy Spirit will fill the entire church. All persevering, all persevering in prayer, all persevering in prayer in one place and then all filled with the Holy Spirit to overflow.

Garoua, 27/03/06,
The 2nd fifty-two-day fast

39
PRAYER AND HOLINESS

A church should have the following in one prayer meeting.

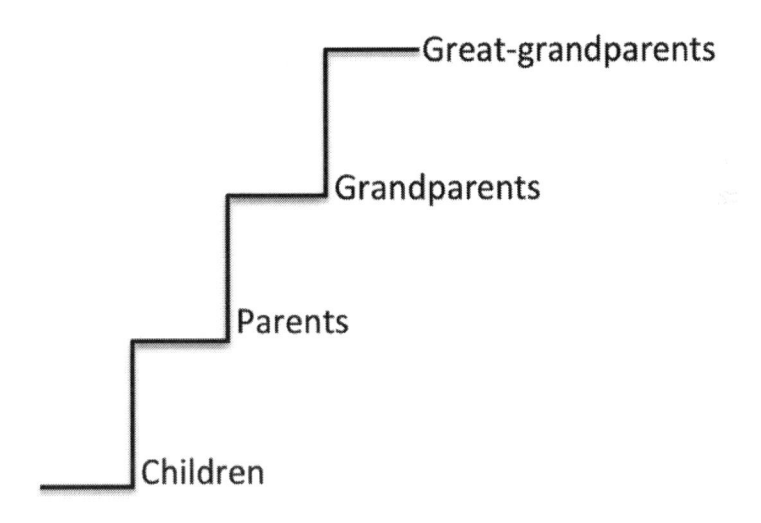

- Great-grandparents
- Grandparents
- Parents
- Children

Such praying of the entire body, will bless each generation present.

Garoua, 27/03/06,
The 2nd fifty-two-day fast

40
PRAYER AND HOLINESS

Prayer demands that the praying one have a clear conscience before God and before man. If there are problems of conscience between man and God or between man and man, the authority, the communion to lay hold of God and to keep laying hold of Him until He answers will be lacking. For some answers to be received from God, entire union and fusion with God are musts.

Garoua, 28/03/06,
The 2nd fifty-two-day fast

41

PRAYER AND HOLINESS

There are those who pray to ease their conscience and all they derive out of the praying is an eased conscience. There are others who pray so that man may know that they have prayed and if man knows that they have prayed, their goal in praying has been achieved. There are others who pray to move God to answer. Such will not utter one word to God before they have ensured that there is no sin of any kind, no disobedience of any kind, no love of the world of any kind, no love of anything that is in the world of any kind that hinders God from hearing and answering them. They are desperate to satisfy the heart of God in everything so that God would answer them fully.

Garoua, 28/03/06,
The 2nd fifty-two-day fast

42

SUSTAINED STAYING IN GOD'S PRESENCE

*I*t is not possible to be free from the shallow life without seventy-two hours, ninety-six hours, one hundred and twenty hours, one hundred and forty-four hours, one hundred and sixty-eight hours, or more of being shut-in with God alone. There are things that God only says to people who spend seventy-two or more hours in His presence continuously.

> *When Moses went up on the mountain, the cloud covered it, and the glory of the Lord settled on Mount Sinai. For six days the cloud covered the mountain, and <u>on the seventh day</u>, the Lord called to Moses from within the cloud* (Exodus 24:15-16).

If Moses had come back from the mountain after six days, he would have heard nothing from God. There are issues that cannot be prayed through on superficial encounters with God. There are issues that cannot be prayed through after a short time in God's presence. For the deeper, broader and higher issues, a person must enter into God's presence and be filled with the presence and power of God, and then and only then can such issues be raised with God.

Yaounde, 05/04/06

43
LEADERSHIP AND PRAYER

The leader has the supreme responsibility of carrying the people he leads to God in prayer.

Johannesburg, 01/05/06,
The 2nd Supra-long fast,
First missionary journey to South Africa

44
LEADERSHIP

The leader has the supreme responsibility of bringing God down in prayer so that He may be in the midst of them. As he prays, he will be filled with the fullness of God and as he moves around, those who come near to him will encounter the fullness of God; his people will live in an atmosphere of the fullness of God.

Johannesburg, 01/05/06,
The 2nd Supra-long fast,
First missionary journey to South Africa

45
LEADERSHIP

If the leader does not take the people to God in prayer, the enemy will take them to the world.

Johannesburg, 01/05/06,
The 2nd Supra-long fast,
First missionary journey to South Africa

46

LEADERSHIP AND PRAYERLESSNESS

If the people whom a person leads backslide, it is because the leader has failed to pray. The prayer of the leader draws the people he leads to God. The prayerlessness of the leader causes the people to fall away, to backslide, to love the world, to be wrapped in the web of self-love and to perish. The prayerlessness of a leader is tragic beyond telling.

Johannesburg, 01/05/06,
The 2nd Supra-long fast,
First missionary journey to South Africa

47
PRAYER

Prayer is the overflow of intimacy with God.

Yaounde, 17/05/06,
The 2nd Supra-long fast

48
PRAYER

Prayer flows from a life that walks with God. Prayer flows from the knowledge of God. Prayer flows from union and communion with God. Only those who plug into God can pray and do pray.

Yaounde, 17/05/06,
The 2nd Supra-long fast

THE MINISTRY OF THANKSGIVING, PRAISE AND WORSHIP

Thanksgiving, praise and worship are to flow from spirit-filled hearts to the Lord Almighty.

His father Zechariah was filled with the Holy Spirit and prophesied: Praise be to the Lord, the God of Israel, because he has come and has redeemed his people (Luke 1:67-68).

***Yaounde, 17/05/06,
The 2nd Supra-long fast***

50

THE MINISTRY OF THANKSGIVING, PRAISE AND WORSHIP

Thanksgiving, praise and worship should be normal. The normal believer should raise his voice and pour out his life in thanksgiving, praise and worship ten, twenty, fifty or one hundred times each day.

Yaounde, 17/05/06,
The 2nd Supra-long fast

51

PRAYER WITH TEARS

*T*ears are a weapon for moving God on behalf of cities and nations.

In those days Hezekiah became ill and was at the point of death. The prophet Isaiah son of Amoz went to him and said, "This is what the LORD says:

> *Put your house in order, because you are going to die; you will not recover." Hezekiah turned his face to the wall and prayed to the LORD, Remember, O LORD, how I have walked before you faithfully and with wholehearted devotion and have done what is good in your eyes. And Hezekiah wept bitterly. Then the word of the LORD came to Isaiah: Go and tell Hezekiah, 'This is what the LORD, the God of your father David, says: I have heard your prayer and seen your tears; I will add fifteen years to your life. And I will deliver you and this city from the hand of the king of Assyria. I will defend this city* (Isaiah 38:1–6).

The words of Nehemiah son of Hacaliah:

In the month of Kislev in the twentieth year, while I was in the citadel of Susa, Hanani, one of my brothers, came from Judah with some other men, and I questioned them about the Jewish remnant that survived the exile, and also about Jerusalem. They said to me, "Those who survived the exile and are back in the province are in great trouble and disgrace. The wall of Jerusalem is broken down, and its gates have been burned with fire." When I heard these things, I sat down and wept. For some days I mourned and fasted and prayed before the God of heaven (Nehemiah 1:1–4).

In bitterness of soul Hannah wept much and prayed to the LORD. And she made a vow, saying, "O LORD Almighty, if you will only look upon your servant's misery and remember me, and not forget your servant but give her a son, then I will give him to the LORD for all the days of his life, and no razor will ever be used on his head." As she kept on praying to the LORD, Eli observed her mouth. Hannah was praying in her heart, and her lips were moving but her voice was not heard. Eli thought she was drunk and said to her, "How long will you keep on getting drunk? Get rid of your wine." Not so, my lord, Hannah replied, "I am a woman who is deeply troubled. I have not been drinking wine or beer; I was pouring out my soul to the LORD. Do not take your servant for a wicked woman; I have been praying here out of my great anguish and grief."

Eli answered, "Go in peace, and may the God of Israel grant you what you have asked of him." She said, "May your servant find favor in your eyes." Then she went her way and ate something, and her face was no longer downcast. Early the next morning they arose and worshiped before the LORD and then went back to their home at Ramah. Elkanah lay with Hannah his wife, and the LORD remembered her.

So in the course of time Hannah conceived and gave birth to a son. She named him Samuel, saying, "Because I asked the LORD for him." When the man Elkanah went up with all his family to offer the annual sacrifice to the LORD and to fulfill his vow, Hannah did not go. She said to her husband, "After the boy is weaned, I will take him and present him before the LORD, and he will live there always." Do what seems best to you, Elkanah her husband told her. "Stay here until you have weaned him; only may the LORD make good his word." So the woman stayed at home and nursed her son until she had weaned him.

After he was weaned, she took the boy with her, young as he was, along with a three-year-old bull, an ephah of flour and a skin of wine, and brought him to the house of the LORD at Shiloh. When they had slaughtered the bull, they brought the boy to Eli, and she said to him, "As surely as you live, my lord, I am the woman who stood here beside you praying to the LORD. I prayed for this child, and the LORD has granted me what I asked of him. So now I give him to the LORD. For his whole life he will be given over to the LORD." And he worshiped the LORD there (1 Samuel 1:10–28).

I served the Lord with great humility and with tears, although I was severely tested by the plots of the Jews (Acts 20:19)

Kinshasa, 19/05/06,
The 2nd Supra-long fast

52
PRAYER WITH TEARS

The hearts of the people cry out to the Lord. O wall of the Daughter of Zion, let your tears flow like a river day and night; give yourself no relief, your eyes no rest. Arise, cry out in the night, as the watches of the night begin; pour out your heart like water in the presence of the Lord. Lift up your hands to him for the lives of your children, who faint from hunger at the head of every street (Lamentations 2:18–19).

Kinshasa, 19/05/06,
The 2nd Supra-long fast

53
BARRIERS TO ANSWER

God takes account not only of what we want, but of why we want it. He looks at the heart. There are some people to whom He will not give audience.

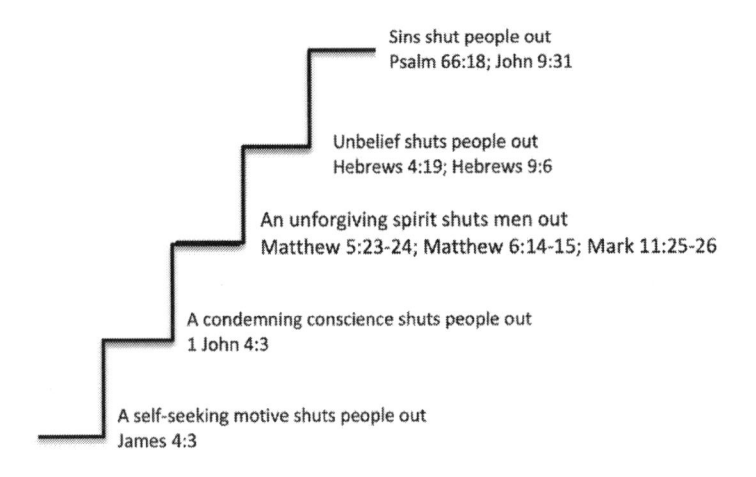

- Sins shut people out
  Psalm 66:18; John 9:31
- Unbelief shuts people out
  Hebrews 4:19; Hebrews 9:6
- An unforgiving spirit shuts men out
  Matthew 5:23-24; Matthew 6:14-15; Mark 11:25-26
- A condemning conscience shuts people out
  1 John 4:3
- A self-seeking motive shuts people out
  James 4:3

Adopted from Samuel Chadwick

***Kinshasa, 19/05/06,
The 2nd Supra-long fast***

54
PRAYER AND HOLINESS

The Holy Spirit cannot intercede in an impure heart. He is the Spirit of holiness and where there is sin, He must remain silent. He cannot deny Himself and pray in an unholy heart.

Yaounde, 24/05/06,
The 2nd Supra-long fast

55

PRAYER AND HOLINESS

The Holy Spirit cannot intercede through an impure heart. Heart Impurity is a choice and those who choose to keep their hearts impure have chosen not to have the Holy Spirit intercede through them.

Yaounde, 24/05/06,
The 2nd Supra-long fast

56

PRAYER

True prayer is the overflow of the Holy Spirit through a Spirit-filled life. In such a person, the Holy Spirit clothes Himself with the human spirit of the Spirit-filled person and causes prayer that originates in the Lord of heaven to flow to God and such prayer is always answered by God the Father.

Nkambe, 11/06/06,
The 2nd Supra-long fast

57
PRAYER

To ask for myself something that the Lord Jesus would not have asked for Himself is unrighteousness.

Nkambe, 01/06.06,
The 2nd Supra-long fast

58
PRAYER AND TEARS

In bitterness of soul Hannah wept much and prayed to the Lord (1 Samuel 1:10).

London, 17/06/06,
The 2nd Supra-long fast

59

PRAYER AND TEARS

There are things that can be received from the Lord by violent praying and if violent praying goes up to the Lord God Almighty, those things will be received. There are other things that can only be received from the Lord through bitter tears. Those who weep bitterly receive those things and those who do not know bitter tears will not receive those things.

> *In those days Hezekiah became ill and was at the point of death. The prophet Isaiah son of Amoz went to him and said, "This is what the LORD says: Put your house in order, because you are going to die; you will not recover." Hezekiah turned his face to the wall and prayed to the LORD, Remember, O LORD, how I have walked before you faithfully and with wholehearted devotion and have done what is good in your eyes. And Hezekiah wept bitterly. Then the word of the LORD came to Isaiah: Go and tell Hezekiah, 'This is what the LORD, the God of your father David, says: I have heard your prayer and seen your tears; I will add fifteen years to your life. And I will deliver you and this city from the hand of the king of Assyria. I will defend this city. 'This is the LORD's sign to*

you that the LORD will do what he has promised: I will make the shadow cast by the sun go back the ten steps it has gone down on the stairway of Ahaz.' " So the sunlight went back the ten steps it had gone down (Isaiah 38:1-8).

London, 17/06/06,
The 2nd Supra-long fast

60
PRAYER AND TEARS

When I heard these things, I sat down and wept. For some days I mourned and fasted and prayed to the God of heaven (Nehemiah 1:4).

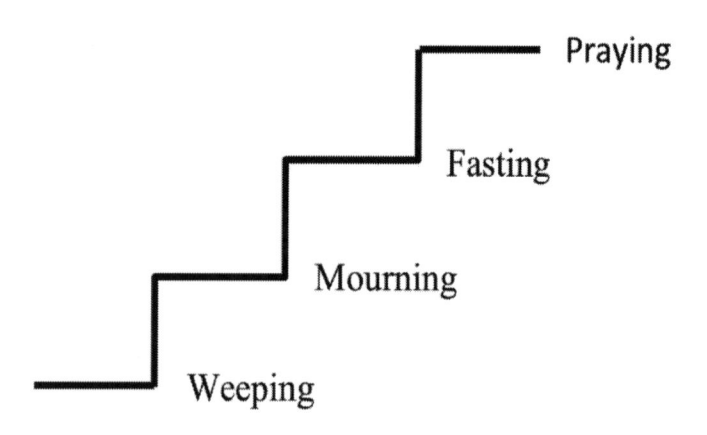

```
                                    ──── Praying
                           ──── Fasting
                  ──── Mourning
         ──── Weeping
```

Tears are the first weapon with which to lay hold of a person, a family, a quarter, a town or city, a nation or a continent for God.

*London, 17/06/06,
The 2nd Supra-long fast*

61
PRAYER AND HUMAN BURDENS

The Apostle Peter said,

Cast all your anxiety on him because he cares for you (1 Peter 5:7).

This is God's command. Not to cast any burden at His feet is disobedience. To carry one burden is sin. Part of the life of prayer is to cast the burdens of man at the feet of the Lord Jesus and so create room for the burdens of God which are carried to Him in prayer, so that the believer is normally burden-free and rejoicing in the Lord.

Yaounde, 29/06/06,
The 2nd Supra-long fast

62

PRAYER AND HUMAN BURDENS

Do not be anxious about anything, but in everything, by prayer and petition, with thanksgiving, present your requests to God. And the peace of God, which transcends all understanding, will guard your hearts and your minds in Christ Jesus (Philippians 4:6–7).

Yaounde, 29/06/06,
The 2nd Supra-long fast

63
PRAYER AND HUMAN BURDENS

What is lifted to God in prayer becomes a burden to be carried.

<u>Prayer is the end of a life crushed by burdens</u>. Prayer changes a man who would have been carrying burdens into a burden-free man carrying the gospel that liberates others.

Yaounde, 29/06/06,
The 2nd Supra-long fast

64
PRAYER AND HUMAN BURDENS

The person who prayerfully lays his burdens at the feet of the Lord Jesus Christ will be free from his burden, and so be free to go and win a crown or crowns to be laid at His feet on Judgement Day.

Yaounde, 29/06/06,
The 2nd Supra-long fast

65
PRAYER AND HYPOCRISY

The hypocrite prays that God should do in another what he has not allowed God to do in him. If a person would want God to do something in another, that one should first of all allow God to do that same thing in his own life and then he can pray that God should do in others what He has done in him.

Yaounde, 29/06/06,
The 2nd Supra-long fast

66
PRAYER AND SOUL-WINNING

Many times, our efforts in leading people to Christ are fruitless. We forget the necessary preparation for witnessing. The divine order is, first to talk to God about man, and then to talk to men about God. If we follow this formula, we shall see results. Prayer is really the place where people are won to Christ; service is just gathering in the results of our prayer.

— BILL BRIGHT IN, *A HANDBOOK FOR CHRISTIAN MATURITY,* HERE'S LIFE PUBLISHERS, SAN BERNADINO, 1982. P17...

Yaounde, 01/07/06,
The 2nd Supra-long fast

67
PRAYER

Prayer is battling with God so that He acts in an emergency.

Yaounde, 05/07/06,
The 2nd Supra-long fast

68
PRAYER

Prayer is calling on the Lord as a woman in the pains of child birth.

Yaounde, 05/07/06,
The 2nd Supra-long fast

69
SUMS FOR GOD'S GLOBAL ENTERPRISES

Those who take upon themselves the responsibility of moving God to give extraordinary large sums to His global enterprise must be people scarred from many a wound received in ordinary and extraordinary giving to God. People living at ease and in indulgence, and praying that God would release extraordinary sums into His global enterprise, are deceived beyond measure.

Yaounde, 05/07/06,
The 2nd Supra-long fast

70
SUMS FOR GOD'S GLOBAL ENTERPRISES

Those who take upon themselves the responsibility of moving God to give extraordinary large sums to His global enterprise must be people who have chosen the pathway of permanent voluntary poverty because of the perishing souls of those for whom the Lord Jesus Christ died. It is not possible to live in luxury, indulgence and ease, and then move God to give extraordinary large sums to His global enterprise. <u>Extreme sacrifices authorize the one who sacrifices to move God to do the near impossible.</u>

Yaounde, 05/07/06,
The 2nd Supra-long fast

71
ANXIETY-FREE CHRISTIANITY

For depths in prayer, a person should come to the Lord Jesus, first of all, and lay at His feet all that causes him weariness. Such a person should lay all his yokes and all his burdens, one after another, on the Lord Jesus until none is left. After that he should lay his burden-free heart at the feet of the Lord Jesus and receive from the Lord Jesus His easy yoke and His light burden and bear these in prayer for Him. The Lord Jesus said,

> *Come to me, all you who are weary and burdened, and I will give you rest. Take my yoke upon you and learn from me, for I am gentle and humble in heart, and you will find rest for your souls. For my yoke is easy and my burden is light* (Mathew 11:28-30).

Depths in prayer are only possible for the person who has entered the rest of God, rest from his own burdens and his own yokes.

Johannesburg, 14/07/06,
The 2nd Supra-long fast

ANXIETY-FREE CHRISTIANITY

Do not be anxious about anything, but in everything, by prayer and petition, with thanksgiving, present your requests to God. And the peace of God, which transcends all understanding, will guard your hearts and your minds in Christ Jesus (Philippians 4:6–7),

Everything capable of causing anxiety must be made a subject of prayer and the prayer must continue until all that is capable of causing anxiety has been thrown away through being laid at the feet of the Lord in prayer.

Cast all your anxiety on him because he cares for you (1 Peter 5:7).

Johannesburg, 14/07/06,
The 2nd Supra-long fast

73
PRAYER

*P*rayer is entering into a covenant with God, that He will be moved to do something or some things, and that the labour to move Him will continue relentlessly until He answers, regardless of how long He takes to do it.

Paris, 28/07/06,
The 2nd Supra-long fast,
The 6th Western Europe Convention

74
PRAYER

Prayer is, first of all, touching God, then it is union, and then it is fusion with God.

Paris, 28/07/06,
The 2nd Supra-long fast,
The 6th Western Europe Convention

75
VICTORIOUS PRAYING

In praying, there are prayer volumes, prayer heights, prayer depths that must be acquired, added to, superseded, so that God is moved to do what only He can do. Without the investment of one's all to acquire the indispensable volumes, heights and depths, one will go away without answers to critical requests.

Yaounde, 01/08/06,
The 2nd Supra-long fast

76
VICTORIOUS PRAYING

Victorious praying is praying to break; praying to melt; praying to explode. A person succeeds in prayer to the extent to which he is prepared to break, to melt and to explode in prayer.

Yaounde, 01/08/06,
The 2nd Supra-long fast

77
PRAYER

There is a law of prayer that demands that a person should not pray that God should do in another what God has not done in the one who wants to pray. To pray that God should do in another what you have not allowed Him do in you is hypocrisy. If a person sees something wrong in another, which he wants God to take away, he must look and find out if that fault is found in himself. If it is found in himself, he must get rid of it completely before he can begin to pray that God would get rid of it in others. If he does not get rid of it but continues to pray that the Lord should do it in others, he is sinning and not walking in the way of the Lord.

Yaounde, 02/08/06,
The 2nd Supra-long fast

78
PRAYER

Progress in prayer depends on progress in God's dealings with the praying one.

To the extent that a person allows God to possess him, can he pray. The more God possesses the praying man, the greater the extent to which he can pray.

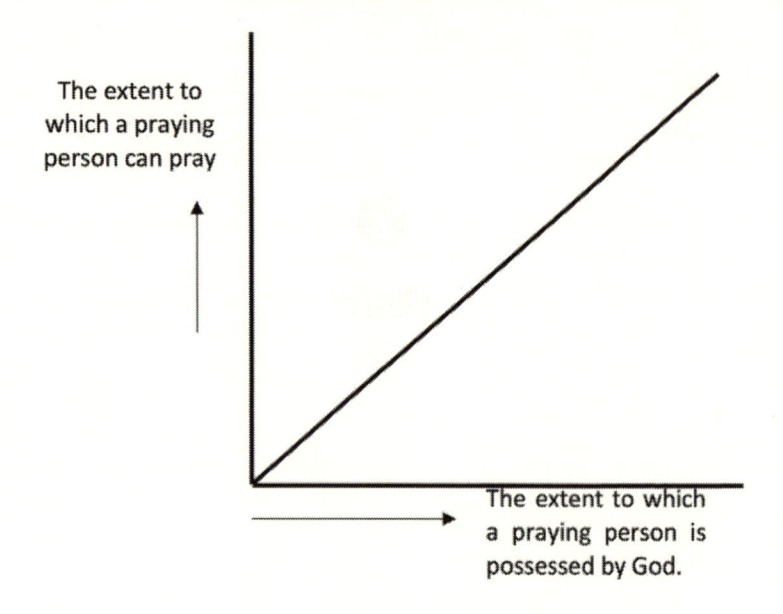

```
         ^
         |
The extent to
which a praying
person can pray
```

(graph: diagonal line rising from origin)

The extent to which a praying person can pray (y-axis)

The extent to which a praying person is possessed by God. (x-axis)

Yaounde, 02/08/06,
The 2nd Supra-long fast

PRAYER

First-class believers are pre-occupied with the needs of God—Father, Son and Holy Spirit, in prayer.

Second class believers are pre-occupied with the needs of other human beings in prayer. Third-class believers are pre-occupied with their own needs in prayer. First class believers pray primarily for the needs and burdens of God. Second class believers pray primarily for the needs and burdens of others. Third-class believers are pre-occupied with their own needs.

Lagos, 05/08/06,
The 2nd Supra-long fast

80
PRAYER

*I*n true prayer, a person plugs into God, stays in God's presence, until God reveals a divine need to him and gives him the divine burden to see that need met. With the need revealed and the burden given, the praying person begins to pray and continues to pray until the burden is discharged. The praying person then departs knowing that the need has been met in the heavenly realm and will soon be manifested in the visible.

Lagos, 05/08/06,
The 2nd Supra-long fast

81
LEADERSHIP

*L*eadership includes the unusual capacity to frequently withdraw to meet God afresh, and so the leader frequently brings something new or fresh from the Lord to the people he leads. Those times of withdrawal are times of union and communion with the Lord.

Lagos, 05/08/06,
The 2nd Supra-long fast

82
PRAYER

During prayer, I must call on God, knowing that if God does not intervene, all will be lost. After praying, I must put in everything to ensure that I co-operate with God to make His intervention possible. After praying, I must invest my all to act for the thing I have asked in prayer to become reality. So prayer is investing everything to move God to act; prayer is doing everything that I can do to co-operate with God so that the answer God gives is received.

Lagos, 05/08/06,
The 2nd Supra-long fast

PRAYER ALONE

Prayer alone is the place of the exchange of burdens. The believer casts his heavy burdens and cares at the feet of the Lord Jesus Christ and receives the Lord's light burdens in exchange for his heavy burdens. The Lord Jesus said,

> *Come to me, all you who are weary and burdened, and I will give you rest. Take my yoke upon you and learn from me, for I am gentle and humble in heart, and you will find rest for your souls. For my yoke is easy and my burden is light* (Mathew 11:28–30).

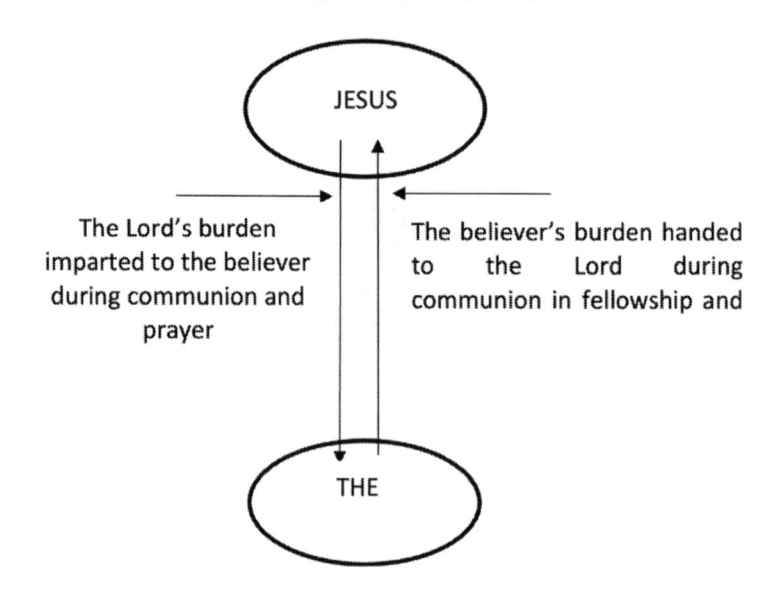

```
                    JESUS
                   ┌──────┐
                   │      │
                   └──┬───┘
                      ↕
  The Lord's burden         The believer's burden handed
  imparted to the believer  to   the   Lord   during
  during communion and      communion in fellowship and
  prayer
                      ↕
                   ┌──────┐
                   │ THE  │
                   └──────┘
```

Kumasi, 12/08/06,
The 2nd Supra-long fast

84
PRAYER ALONE

Prayer alone is heart union and heart fusion between the Lord God Almighty and His earthly lover—the believer in the Lord Jesus. During prayer alone, God opens His heart without reservations to His lover, and the earthly lover stands before his Heavenly Beloved transparent, so that intimacy reaches increasing intensity with passing time. Because this is so, sessions of prayer alone need more and more time with increasing relationship—a few minutes pass into many minutes, a few hours, many hours, very many hours and perhaps days and weeks.

Kumasi, 12/08/06,
The 2nd Supra-long fast

85
PRAYER ALONE

Times of prayer alone are times of spiritual ecstasy. The Heavenly Beloved and the earthly lover come into union and communion and the place of prayer becomes heaven on earth.

Kumasi, 12/08/06,
The 2nd Supra-long fast

86
PRAYER AND LEADERSHIP

Leadership is constraining those led to be involved with the leader in his battles,

- experiences,
- victories,
- trials,
- exploits,
- others.

Leadership constrains the people through prayer and fasting. As the leader fasts and prays for the people he leads, God will work in them to move them to become involved with the leader in his battles, experiences, victories, trials, exploits, and so on.

Yaounde, 23/08/06,
The 2nd Supra-long fast

87
PRAYER

The place of prayer is the place for the holy. It is the place where the holy one(s) lay(s) hold of the All-Holy One.

Yaounde, 23/08/06,
The 2nd Supra-long fast

88
PRAYER AND HOLINESS

The abandonment of all sin forever is the minimum level of holiness required of anyone who wants to pray.

Yaounde, 23/08/06,
The 2nd Supra-long fast

89

PRAYER AND HOLINESS

The place of prayer is the place of utter holiness.

Yaounde, 23/08/06,
The 2nd Supra-long fast

90
PRAYER AND HOLINESS

Prayer is the overflow of a holy heart, to a holy God.

Yaounde, 23/08/06,
The 2nd Supra-long fast

91
PRAYER AND HOLINESS

- The prayer room is the place of holiness.
- The prayer chain is the chain of holiness.
- The prayer crusade is the crusade of holiness.
- The prayer siege is the siege of holiness.
- The prayer movement is the movement of holiness.

Yaounde, 23/08/06,
The 2nd Supra-long fast

92

PRAYER AND HOLINESS

Every sin is committed or entertained as a matter of choice; it can be rejected immediately, and a life of holiness entered into and dwelt in, thus opening the way to true prayer.

Yaounde, 23/08/06,
The 2nd Supra-long fast

93
PRAYER ALONE

The believer is a lover of the Lord who seeks for more and more intimacy with the Lord. The believer-lover hungers to behold the Lord's face and this can only be shown to him in secret. So prayer alone is absolutely indispensable to such a one because the deeper things are done by the Lord in secret. Prayer alone is the place of that secrecy. The Lord Jesus said,

> *But when you pray, go into your room, close the door and pray to your Father, who is unseen. Then your Father, who sees what is done in secret, will reword you* (Mathew 6:6).

Kumasi, 23/08/06,
The 2nd Supra-long fast

94
PRAYER

At the place of prayer, alone with God, the inner recesses of a person are exposed to the Holy Spirit, and He carries out the work of cleansing, deepening, broadening and heightening.

Bangui, 15/09/06,
The 2nd Supra-long fast,
The 6th missionary journey to Bangui

95
PRAYER

The place of prayer is the place where heaven and earth meet. At the place of prayer, an honest heart abandons all sin and all hypocrisy and becomes bare and true before God. The supplicant opens his heart to God and God puts His burden on the heart of the supplicant. Then the supplicant utters the burden as a supplication to God and thus the burden of God is presented to Him from the earth. God's answer establishes the will of heaven on earth. This is prayer.

Bangui, 15/09/06,
The 2nd Supra-long fast,
The 6th missionary journey to Bangui

96
PRAYER

*P*rayerlessness is a plague—a deadly plague that destroys husbands, wives, children, quarters, cities, nations and entire continents.

Yaounde, 04/10/06,
The 2nd Supra-long fast,
The Determinant Prayer Crusade – 2006

97
PRAYER

There is a relationship between an individual's praying alone and the individual's praying with others. The person who prays much alone will also labour to pray much with others.

Yaounde, 04/10/06,
The 2nd Supra-long fast,
The Determinant Prayer Crusade – 2006

PRAYER AND CONSECRATION

*P*rayer is, first of all, a life offered in utter consecration to the Lord Jesus and then supplications offered in His Name to God the Father.

Yaounde, 06/10/06,
The 2nd Supra-long fast,
The Determinant Prayer Crusade - 2006

99
PRAYER

You are my war club, my weapon for battle—with you I shatter nations, with you I destroy kingdoms, with you I shatter horse and rider, with you I shatter chariot and driver, with you I shatter man and woman, with you I shatter old man and youth, with you I shatter young man and maiden, with you I shatter shepherd and flock, with you I shatter farmer and oxen, with you I shatter governors and officials (Jeremiah 51:20–23).

Yaounde, 06/10/06,
The 2nd Supra-long fast,
The Determinant Prayer Crusade – 2006

100
PRAYER

Prayer must flow from holiness—continuous holiness.

Yaounde, 12/10/06,
The 2nd Supra-long fast,
The Determinant Prayer Crusade – 2006

101
PRAYER

Prayer must flow from a walk with God.

Yaounde, 12/10/06,
The 2nd Supra-long fast,
The Determinant Prayer Crusade – 2006

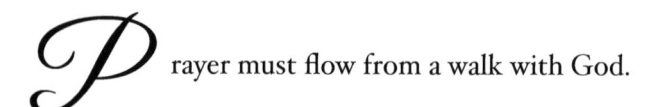

PRAYER AND HOLINESS - PRAYER AND OBEDIENCE

If I close my ears to the Lord God Almighty about one thing, He will close His ears to all my prayers, to all my supplications and to all my intercessions. This means that if I disobey God in one thing, He will "disobey" me in all that I ask of Him.

Yaounde, 12/10/06,
The 2nd Supra-long fast,
The Determinant Prayer Crusade - 2006

103
PRAYER AND HOLINESS

*I*t takes only one sin committed intentionally and the relationship with God is broken permanently.

Yaounde, 12/10/06,
The 2nd Supra-long fast,
The Determinant Prayer Crusade - 2006

104
PRAYER AND LEADERSHIP

Leadership is provided by praying alone and by praying with others.

Yaounde, 12/10/06,
The 2nd Supra-long fast,
The Determinant Prayer Crusade - 2006

105
PRAYER AND LEADERSHIP

A person who does not distinguish himself in praying alone and in praying with others has failed in leadership.

Yaounde, 12/10/06,
The 2nd Supra-long fast,
The Determinant Prayer Crusade - 2006

106
PRAYER AND LEADERSHIP

*L*eadership in prayer is leadership in moving God to answer. The leader is the one who moves God to answer as no one else can move Him. This power to move God to act is the central ingredient in leadership.

Yaounde, 14/10/06,
The 2nd Supra-long fast,
The Determinant Prayer Crusade – 2006

107
PRAYER AND HOLINESS

Words of repentance in prayer that do not flow from a repentant heart are an abomination before God.

Yaounde, 14/10/06,
The 2nd Supra-long fast,
The Determinant Prayer Crusade – 2006

108
VIOLENT PRAYING

The enemy understands only the language of violence. He labours to resist each believer full scale. Only those who come against him in violent prayer, violent fasting, violent holiness and violent giving to the Lord will knock him off consistently and establish the kingdom of the Lord Jesus Christ as it should be. The praying man is a warrior and the place of prayer is the battle front. The enemy is there and so is the believer. The nonviolent believer has already lost the battle. The violent believer wins.

Yaounde, 17/10/06,
The 2nd Supra-long fast,
The Determinant Prayer Crusade – 2006

109
VIOLENT PRAYING

There can be no violence without the expenditure of energy. Violent praying demands the expenditure of massive quantities of energy. The person who chooses to spare himself the expenditure of massive quantities of energy in prayer has also chosen to limit his prayers significantly.

Yaounde, 17/10/06,
The 2nd Supra-long fast,
The Determinant Prayer Crusade - 2006

110
THE MINISTRY OF TEARS

Oh, that my head were a spring of water and my eyes a fountain of tears! I would weep day and night for the slain of my people (Jeremiah 9:1).

Paris, 22/10/06,
The 2nd Supra-long fast,
The Determinant Prayer Crusade - 2006

HEARING GOD'S VOICE AND CO-OPERATING WITH HIM

What God has said to me must be. To hear God's voice and refuse to co-operate with Him so that what He has said comes to pass is great wickedness. My Lord, I have committed the sin of great wickedness very many times. O Lord, forgive me.

Paris, 24/10/06,
The 2nd Supra-long fast,
The Determinant Prayer Crusade - 2006

112
THE MINISTRY OF TEARS

This is what the LORD Almighty says:

"Consider now! Call for the wailing women to come; send for the most skillful of them.

Let them come quickly and wail over us till our eyes overflow with tears and water streams from our eyelids. The sound of wailing is heard from Zion: 'How ruined we are! How great is our shame! We must leave our land because our houses are in ruins.' " Now, O women, hear the word of the LORD; open your ears to the words of his mouth. Teach your daughters how to wail; teach one another a lament (Jeremiah 9:17–20).

Paris, 24/10/06,
The 2nd Supra-long fast,
The Determinant Prayer Crusade – 2006

113
THE MINISTRY OF TEARS

Streams of tears flow from my eyes because my people are destroyed. My eyes will flow unceasingly, without relief, until the LORD looks down from heaven and sees (Lamentations 3:48-50).

Paris, 25/10/06,
The 2nd Supra-long fast,
The Determinant Prayer Crusade - 2006

114
THE MINISTRY OF TEARS

The hearts of the people cry out to the Lord. O wall of the Daughter of Zion, let your tears flow like a river day and night; give yourself no relief, your eyes no rest. Arise, cry out in the night, as the watches of the night begin; pour out your heart like water in the presence of the Lord. Lift up your hands to him for the lives of your children, who faint from hunger at the head of every street (Lamentations 2:18–19).

Paris, 25/10/06,
The 2nd Supra-long fast,
The Determinant Prayer Crusade – 2006

115

PRAYER AND HOLINESS

The only prayers that dismantle the kingdom of Satan are those that flow from pure and holy hearts. Prayer that flows from sin-tarnished hearts have no impact on the enemy's kingdom. They are hindered by the sin of the praying on

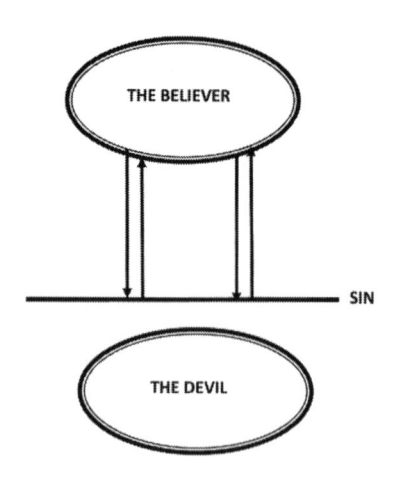

```
        ┌─────────────┐
        │ THE BELIEVER │
        └─────────────┘
           ↕      ↕
    ━━━━━━━━━━━━━━━━━━━━ SIN
        ┌─────────────┐
        │  THE DEVIL   │
        └─────────────┘
```

Ouagadougou, 04/11/06,

The 2nd Supra-long fast,
The Determinant Prayer Crusade – 2006

ANSWERS TO PRAYER

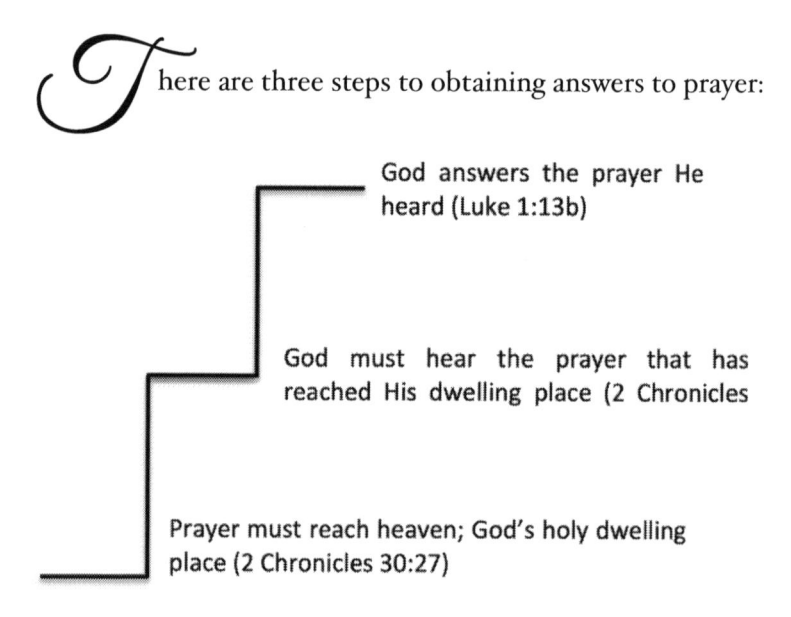

There are three steps to obtaining answers to prayer:

- God answers the prayer He heard (Luke 1:13b)

- God must hear the prayer that has reached His dwelling place (2 Chronicles

- Prayer must reach heaven; God's holy dwelling place (2 Chronicles 30:27)

Maputo, 15/11/06,
The 2nd Supra-long fast,
The Determinant Prayer Crusade – 2006

117
PRAYER

The important thing about prayer is that it reaches God, is heard and answered. Praying for any other reason is a great waste of time. Praying that does not involve the putting in of a man's all is joking and deceit. It may demand nine hours of preparation to pray for one hour that will move God to answer.

Maputo, 15/11/06,
The 2nd Supra-long fast,
The Determinant Prayer Crusade - 2006

118
PRAYER WITH TEARS

It is impossible to work and witness for Christ with cold hearts and dry eyes. Christians must be taught the importance of having a closet, the floor of which is worn by hard praying and ever wet with tears.

— HERBERT LOCKYER, *HERALD OF HIS COMING*, VOLUME 12, NO. 1, 1952, PAGE 5

Yaounde, 09/12/06,
The 2nd Supra-long fast,
The Determinant Prayer Crusade - 2006

119
PRAYER WITH TEARS

*H*ezekiah *turned his face to the wall and prayed to the LORD,*

"Remember, O LORD, how I have walked before you faithfully and with wholehearted devotion and have done what is good in your eyes." And Hezekiah wept bitterly.

Before Isaiah had left the middle court, the word of the LORD came to him: Go back and tell Hezekiah, the leader of my people, 'This is what the LORD, the God of your father David, says: I have heard your prayer and seen your tears; I will heal you. On the third day from now you will go up to the temple of the LORD (2 Kings 20:2-5).

Yaounde, 09/12/06,
The 2nd Supra-long fast,
The Determinant Prayer Crusade – 2006

120
PRAYER AND TRUE CONVERSION

True conversion takes place when God is moved by prayer and fasting to come down from heaven, and overwhelm the sinner so that the sinner hates all sin, all self, all love of the world, all love of all the things that are in the world, departs from them in a radical and total way and hungers for God with a hunger that can only cease when the sinner has carried out true repentance towards God, and exercised genuine faith in the Lord Jesus.

Falambougou - Mali, 16/12/06,
The 2nd Supra-long fast

121
THE MINISTRY OF TEARS

*I*n the walk with God, at the point of deepest union and fusion with the Lord, there comes a point where words are no longer the vehicle for flowing to God. Tears become the weapon through which the Holy Spirit flows to God in co-operation with the believer. Such praying, the prayers with tears, reach God in power as was the case of King Hezekiah. The Bible says,

> *In those days Hezekiah became ill and was at the point of death. The prophet Isaiah son of Amoz went to him and said, "This is what the LORD says: Put your house in order, because you are going to die; you will not recover." Hezekiah turned his face to the wall and prayed to the LORD, Remember, O LORD, how I have walked before you faithfully and with wholehearted devotion and have done what is good in your eyes. And Hezekiah wept bitterly. Then the word of the LORD came to Isaiah: Go and tell Hezekiah, 'This is what the LORD, the God of your father David, says: I have heard your prayer and seen your tears; I will add fifteen years to your life. And I will deliver you and this city from the hand of the king of Assyria. I will defend this city.' This is the LORD's sign to*

you that the LORD will do what he has promised: I will make the shadow cast by the sun go back the ten steps it has gone down on the stairway of Ahaz.' " So the sunlight went back the ten steps it had gone down (Isaiah 38:1-8).

Ndjamena, 20/01/07,
The 2nd Supra-long fast

122
THE MINISTRY OF TEARS

*T*ears flow at moments of deepest union with God, sustained intimacy with God, heights of joy, depths of sorrow or desperation because of need. Tears are another way of flowing to the Lord, of stretching out to reach out to God, of union and communion with Him and another kind of prayer to Him.

Ndjamena, 20/01/07,
The 2nd Supra-long fast

123
SILENCE

God speaks only in silence.

Mother Teresa,
Journey to Yaounde from Ndjamena, 21/01/07

124
PRAYER AND SILENCE

I always begin prayer in silence, for it is in the silence of the heart that God speaks. God is the friend of silence. We need to listen to God because it is not what we say but what He says to us that matters.

Mother Teresa,
Journey to Yaounde from Ndjamena, 21/01/07

PRAYER AND HOLINESS: POSSESSIONS AND PRAYER

Anything that a person possesses and hordes beyond the barest minimum while people are going to hell, who could have been reached were there additional funds, is possessed to the detriment of his inner relationship with the Lord. The things of the world choke the life of God in the believer and paralyse his prayer life. The paralysis does not need to be total. Some praying can still be done and some answers received, but unless there is total identification with the Lord in not loving anything that is in the world, the anointing to

"receive from Him anything we ask" (1 John 3:22)

will be lacking.

Yaounde, 23/01- 07
The 2nd Supra-long fast

126
PRAYER

The discharge of God's special burdens in prayer is determinant praying.

Yaounde, 23/01/07,
The 2nd Supra-long fast

127
DETERMINANT PRAYING

The believer ought to love the Lord and out of that love, spend time in God's presence increasingly, carrying out general praying. As general praying is carried out intensively and extensively, the Lord may then choose this praying one, who has so spent time in His presence doing general or routine praying, to be a special partner with Him. When the Lord chooses someone as His special partner, He will lay on that one, one more of His own special burdens for prayer. In the discharge of this or these special burden(s) of God, determinant praying is done.

Yaounde, 23/01/07,
The 2nd Supra-long fast

128
WALKING WITH GOD

To walk with God is to hear His voice in each situation and to obey Him immediately. The Lord Jesus said,

> *My sheep listen to my voice; I know them, and they follow me* (John 10:27).

The foremost place where the voice of God is heard is at the place of prayer. Prayer is also the place where strength is received to obey immediately.

Yaounde, 25/01/07,
The 2nd Supra-long fast

129
WALKING WITH GOD

To walk with God is to settle in the heart that one will wait on God and keep waiting on God until His voice is heard; for without God's voice heard, where would one walk to? In prayer the resolution not to follow one's voice is made and remade. In prayer the joy of waiting on God is received. In prayer the folly of going ahead of Him or lagging behind Him is seen most clearly so that the praying one says to himself, *"I must wait because not waiting is against Him, against others and against myself."*

Yaounde, 25/01/07,
The 2nd Supra-long fast

130
PRAYER ALONE

*P*rayer alone is the most determinant issue in the relationship with God.

It is at the place of prayer alone that the believer and God fuse and each gives himself to the other. God gives Himself to the praying believer and the praying believer gives himself to God.

Malabo, 27/01/07,
The 2nd Supra-long fast

131

TRUE CONVERSION

True conversion begins at the place of prayer. When a person or persons begin to pray that the Holy Spirit would touch an individual or individuals, there the work begins.

Jos, 03/02/07,
The 2nd Supra-long fast

CONCLUDING THE THIRD MISSIONARY JOURNEY TO MONROVIA

In prayer the all of the praying person must be put in. The person who does not pray with all his might, has decided not to pray at all. The Lord Jesus prayed with "loud cries and tears" (Hebrews 5:7). Only people who pray with all their might, all the time, can prevail with God all the time.

Monrovia, 24/02/07,
The 2nd Supra-long fast

CONCLUDING THE SECOND SUPRA-LONG FAST

I decide, the Lord being my Helper, never again to sleep at the place of prayer, because sleeping at the place of prayer and sleeping during prayer is a choice.

Mbanjock, 08/03/07,
Consolidating the 2nd Supra-long fast

134
LEADERSHIP AND PRAYER

There are those who see what the enemy has done, is doing and will do. Such fear, tremble, and complain. Those who do not pray, or who pray little, concentrate on what the devil and man are doing. Those who pray and pray and concentrate on prayer, concentrate on God, see what God is doing, and are thus strengthened, encouraged and rejoicing. The leader who prays and prays and prays inspires others, and is bold and courageous, whereas the prayerless leader is concentrating on man and on the situation, and from these reaps discouragement.

Douala, 13/04/07,
The 3rd Supra-long fast

135
PRAYER AND THE KNOWLEDGE OF GOD

*P*rayer flows from the knowledge of God. The person who does not know God cannot pray. The person who knows God only a little cannot pray much. The person who knows God a little but pretends to pray much by reciting words and phrases at the place of prayer is doing harm. A person can only pray abundantly out of an abundant knowledge of God.

Yaounde, 17/04/07

136
PRAYER AND HOLINESS

The place of prayer is the place where haters of self-will cry out to God, labouring to move Him to impose His will on their lives, on the church, and on the world.

Yaounde, 17/04/07

137
PRAYER

The place of Prayer is that place in which hearts that flow to the Lord and to each other ask and receive the things that God has in store for them.

Yaounde, 17/04/07

138

PRAYER AND HOLINESS

The prayers of the lazy and the lazy prayers of the hard working have no place before God. There are two main reasons for this: The first is that the throne of God is a throne of holiness. That which is lazy and that which flows from the lazy are sinful and cannot be allowed into God's holy presence.

> *The priests and the Levites stood to bless the people, and God heard them, for their prayer reached heaven, his holy dwelling-place* (2 Chronicles 30:27).

Yaounde, 19/04/07

139

PRAYER AND THE BELIEVERS' CURRENT WEALTH

*A*ll that God has purchased for the believers in Christ is brought from heaven to earth by prayer. Heaven has all that is needed, but it must be brought down by prayer. What is received by the saints on earth is that portion of the total wealth available for them in heaven that has been prayed down.

Yaounde, 19/04/07

140
PRAY WITHOUT CEASING

If a person prays for one hour, he has watched before God for one hour. If that one does not pray for the rest of the twenty-three hours of that day, they have given the devil twenty-three hours to destroy. Thus, there is one hour of watching twenty-three hours of destruction by the enemy. There is only one solution, and that solution is to pray without ceasing. The Bible commands,

Pray continually (1 Thessalonians 5:17).

Yaounde, 19/04/07

141
PRAYER ALONE

Prayer alone is the place of reality. Those who do not know God cannot really pray alone, unless they are in great difficulties. However, for those who know God, the place of prayer is the sweetest place on earth, for in the place of prayer the earthly lover and heavenly Beloved meet and fuse, and the union and fusion has eternal consequence, for the creature flows with longing to the Creator, the Creator flows with supplies to the creature and there is mutual fulfilment. The longing of the creature and the supply of the Creator is Himself.

Yaounde, 20/04/07,
The 56th Retreat,
The 3rd Supra-long fast

PRAY OR PERISH

I am nothing. I am less than nothing. Unless God steps into a situation, all will go wrong. I do not want anything to go wrong. I will pray, I will pray unceasingly, I will get people to pray. I will get them to pray unceasingly. <u>Prayer is the unchanging daily must of my life and ministry.</u>

Yaounde, 23/04/07

143
OBEY OR PERISH

*I*f I do not obey the Lord in one thing that He has commanded me, I have rejected His leadership in all things. He has commanded me to overthrow the hosts of Hinduism, Buddhism and Malsi. Unless I carry out this task, I have rejected His leadership. I must obey or perish.

Yaounde, 23/04/07,
The 56th Retreat,
The 3rd Supra-long fast

144
LEADERSHIP AND PRAYER

Because leadership has to ensure that people are converted from deep-seated interest in people to deep-seated interest in God, the leader must be a man or woman of prayer. Without the effective use of the weapon of prayer, the leader will not be able to ensure that man-centred people are transformed into God-centred people.

Yaounde, 23/04/07,
The 56th ZTF Retreat

145

SPIRITUAL LEADERSHIP AND PRAYER

*P*rayer is the one thing the leader cannot delegate. He must delegate all other things in order to give time to the one thing that he cannot delegate—**prayer.** The twelve apostles said, "*It would not be right for us to neglect the ministry of the word of God in order to wait on tables.*

Brothers, choose seven men from among you who are known to be full of the Spirit and wisdom. We will turn this responsibility over to them *and will give our attention to prayer and the ministry of the word.*"

> So the word of God spread. The number of disciples in Jerusalem increased rapidly, and a large number of priests became obedient to the faith (Acts 6:2b-4,7).

Yaounde, 25/04/07

146
PRAYER AND SOUL-WINNING

The praying of a victorious church should centre on evangelism, soul-winning and church planting.

Kampala, 30/04/07,
The 3rd Supra-long fast

147
PRAYER AND SOUL-WINNING: FASTING AND SOUL-WINNING

The quality and quantity of souls won and kept is determined by the quality and quantity of fasting and prayer that is invested before, during and after the evangelism, soul-winning and church-planting activity. The praying brings down the Holy Spirit, the fasting binds the Devil and then the evangelism, soul-winning and church-planting goes on in the power of the Holy Spirit who works in the preacher and in the one being evangelized. Glory be to the Lord.

Mbale, 04/05/07,
The 2nd missionary journey to Mbale,
The 3rd Supra-long fast

148

PRAYER AND THE OPENING OF THE EYES FOR SEEING

*P*eople are what they are because they do not see:

But they were kept from recognizing him (Luke 24:16).

Then their eyes were opened and they recognized him,

... (Luke 24:31). *Then he opened their minds so that they could understand the Scriptures* (Luke 24:45).

And Elisha prayed,

"O LORD, open his eyes so that he may see" (2 Kings 6:17a).

When people are prayed for, their eyes will be opened and they will see the Lord Jesus and see the world as it is and the response will be entirely different. When Elisha prayed that the Lord should open the eyes of his servant, God opened his eyes and he saw. *Then the LORD opened the servant's eyes, and he looked and saw the hills full of horses and chariots of fire all round Elisha* (2 kings 6:17b).

*Mbale, 04/05/07,
The 2nd missionary journey to Mbale,
The 3rd Supra-long fast*

149
PRAYER AND THE MINISTRY OF THE WORD

When the truth is taught, it must be heard, understood, believed, and lived out. It takes an act of God in answer to prayer, for the hearing, understanding, believing and living out the truth taught, to be what God meant it to be. If there is failure in prayer or too little or feeble praying, the truth taught may fail to be lived out. Prayer is indispensable for making the teaching ministry effective. Prayer is indispensable for an effective teaching ministry.

Kampala, 05/05/07,
The 3rd Supra-long fast

150
PRAYER

For the word of God is living and active. Sharper than any double-edged sword, it penetrates even to dividing soul and spirit, joints and marrow; it judges the thoughts and attitudes of the heart (Hebrews 4:12)

The word that comes out of the mouth of the minister of the word can be received as living and active, sharper than any double-edge sword that penetrates even to the dividing of soul and spirit, joints and marrows, judging the thoughts and attitudes of the heart or as empty and powerless words. The difference is made in the place of prayer. When the minster of the word is a man of prayer and is heavily prayed for, the word will come out of his lips in power and be received as the word of power. If the minster of the word is a man who does not pray or who prays poorly and is not prayed for or poorly prayed for, the word will come forth in weakness.

Kampala, 05/05/07,
The 3rd Supra-long fast

151
PRAYER AND HOLINESS

Prayer is the place of examining the heart before God. When a person comes before God, He should ask the Lord to show him what in his life does not please God. As the Lord shows the things, one after another, they should be confessed and forsaken. When all has been confessed and forsaken, and on pleading with God nothing else is revealed, then there is God's approval that the heart can now pray and be heard.

Kampala, 06/05/07,
The 3rd Supra-long fast

152
PRAYER AND HOLINESS

*I*t takes only one sin committed, known but not repented of and forsaken, for prayer to become noise. Prayer cannot rise to God beyond the holiness of the one praying.

Kampala, 06/05/07,
The 3rd Supra-long fast

153
PRAYER AND SOUL-WINNING

To expect new move in soul-winning without a new move in prayer is to prioritize human action and not divine intervention. There may be no impact at all.

Yaounde, 09/05/07,
The 3rd Supra-long fast

154
PRAYER AND SOUL-WINNING

*I*ntensive and extensive evangelism that flows from intensive and extensive prayer will cause quality and quantity soul-winning to take place.

Yaounde, 09/05/07,
The 3rd Supra-long fast

155
PRAYER AND SOUL-WINNING

There is a veil in the mind of the unbeliever. He cannot understand the gospel until that veil is removed. He may hear the gospel, but he cannot understand because his mind is darkened by the veil. Prayer will move God to tear off the veil, so that the unbeliever can understand the gospel. Prayer is thus a crucial weapon for the soul-winner without which he cannot succeed.

London, 11/05/07,
The 3rd Supra-long fast

156 THANKSGIVING

Always giving thanks to God the Father for everything, in the name of our Lord Jesus Christ (Ephesians 5:20).

London, 11/05/07,
The 3rd Supra-long fast

157
THANKSGIVING

*T*hanksgiving puts an end to a multitude of sins including:

1. Sexual immorality
2. Jealousy
3. Envy
4. Complaining
5. Comparison
6. Bitterness
7. Self-Pity
8. Theft
9. Discouragement
10. Frustration
11. Lying
12. Self-exaltation
13. Anger
14. Slander
15. Spite
16. Selfishness.

London, 12/05/07,
The 3rd Supra-long fast

158
THANKSGIVING

Thanksgiving must become a way of life. Thanksgiving must become a way of life.

London, 12/05/07,
The 3rd Supra-long fast

159
PRAYER AND LEADERSHIP

The leader prays the people he leads into becoming what he wants them to become. If the people are not yet what he wants them to be, the leader must continue to battle in prayer. When he wins in prayer, the people he leads will become what he wants them to become.

Theni, 21/05/07,
7th missionary journey to India,
The 3rd Supra-long fast

160
PRAYER AND LEADERSHIP

The spiritual leader must by prayer, rend the heavens so that the Holy Spirit should come upon and upon his ministry. It is not enough that he prays for the Holy Spirit to come upon him. He must also labour in prayer for the Holy Spirit to come upon his ministry. This will produce a life of power and a ministry of power.

Theni, 21/05/07,
7th missionary journey to India,
The 3rd Supra-long fast

161
HUNGER FOR GOD

The power to hunger after God must be received from God in answer to prayer.

Theni, 21- 05/07,
7th missionary journey to India,
The 3rd Supra-long fast

162
FASTING

I choose to pray more and more. I choose to pray in season and out of season. I choose to fast more and more. I choose to carry out prayer crusades of ever-increasing intensity and ever-increasing duration. I choose to carry out fasts of ever-increasing durations and ever-increasing frequency.

Visakhapatnam, 25/05/07,
Concluding the 3rd Supra-long fast

163
FASTING

That which is born of the flesh is flesh; and that which is born of the Spirit is spirit (John 3:7, KJV).

I have to ask of everything: *"Is this of God or is it of the flesh? Is it of the Holy Spirit or is it of human nature?"* That which is of human nature cannot satisfy the heart of God. Only that which is done through moving God to act is of the Holy Spirit. God can be moved to act by prayer, fasting and all activities that are entirely dependent on the Lord Almighty for its energy. When the Holy Spirit moves into action, God moves in. When the Holy Spirit stays out, God stays out. God can stay out and the flesh continues. God forbid. I must not only pray I must pray Spirit-moved and Spirit-led praying.

I must not only fast. I must carry out Spirit-moved and Spirit-led fasting. It is then that the will of God will be done. It is then that the work of God will be done. All else is wood, hay and stubble. All that originates from my human nature cannot build the Kingdom of God.

Visakhapatnam, 26/05/07
Concluding the 3rd Supra-long fast

164
IMPACT OF PRAYER AND FASTING

I must become a man of prayer and fasting as never before. In prayer and fasting the flesh is weakened and the spirit released and strengthened to bring forth that which is of the Holy Spirit. *"O Lord, I plead with You, enable me to pray as I have never prayed. O Lord enable me to fast as I have never fasted. Glory be to Your Holy Name."*

Visakhapatnam, 26/05/07,
Concluding the 3rd Supra-long fast

165
PRAYER

Prayer is the place where God and man meet and fuse and, in the fusion, God gives Himself to man. The persons who pray intensively and extensively and linger in God's presence, God gives them Himself, whereas those who come to God for short periods receive the things He gives. So the passer-by may receive things from God but the person who dwells in God's presence has God.

Yaounde, 01/06/07,
4th General Course of the World University of Prayer

166
PRAYER

*P*rayer is God's weapon for tearing off the veil that the wicked one has placed on the hearts of the unbelievers.

Yaounde, 01/06/07,
4th General Course of the World University of Prayer,
The 3rd Supra-long fast

167
PRAYER

<u>Prayer is the discharge of a God-given burden</u>. When a person plugs into God, he must remain plugged in so that God would pour His burden on the heart of the person plugged into Him. It may take minutes, hours, days, months and even years for God's burden to be communicated or transferred from God to the one who is plugged into Him, but for the mature saint, staying plugged into God is a way of life.

Yaounde, 01/06/07,
4th General Course of the World University of Prayer

SOUL-WINNING AND PRAYER

No one can come to me unless the Father who sent me draws him (John 6:44A). The Father draws people to the Lord Jesus Christ in answer to prayer. If there is no praying, the Father will not draw anyone to the Lord Jesus Christ.

Yaounde, 01/06/07,
4th General Course of the World University of Prayer,
The 3rd Supra-long fast

169
PRAYER

Only desperate men and women can pray the prayers that compel God to answer. The non-desperate can do without God's intervention and so God does not disturb them with answers.

Nairobi, 08/06/07,
The 3rd Supra-long fast

170
PRAYER

Only those who cannot do without answers from God can really pray, for true prayer is the heart-cry of a desperate man. The person who is desperate will labour and ensure that all possible blocks to his prayer being answered are removed.

Nairobi, 08/06/07,
The 3rd Supra-long fast

171

DESPERATION IN PRAYER

It is desperation in prayer, continuous desperation in prayer, and unceasing prayers, that will move God to do those things that can only be done in answer to desperate praying.

Nairobi, 08/06/07,
The 3rd Supra-long fast

172
DESPERATION IN PRAYER

Desperate prayers flow from inward pain and from inward anguish. Without pain and anguish, a person can pray loudly and noisily but has not prayed desperately.

Nairobi, 08/06/07,
The 3rd Supra-long fast

173
PRAYER AND HOLINESS

This is the confidence we have in approaching God: that if we ask anything according to his will, he hears us (1 John 5:14).

It is imperative for prayers to receive divine approval that they are according to God's will.

Nairobi, 09/06/07

174
PRAYER AND HOLINESS

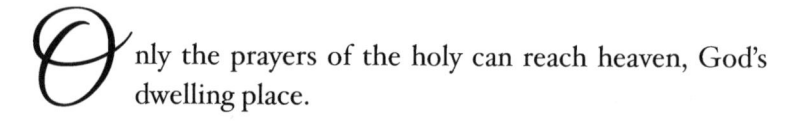

Only the prayers of the holy can reach heaven, God's dwelling place.

The priests and the Levites stood to bless the people, and God heard them, <u>for their prayer reached heaven, his holy dwelling place</u> (2 Chronicles 30:27).

Nairobi, 09/06/07

175
PRAYER AND HOLINESS

The first thing in prayer is to be qualified to pray. This qualification is, first of all, utter separation from all sin permanently. The second is doing the things that please God.

Nairobi, 09/06/07

176
PRAYER

Failure in the proclamation of the word of the Lord is first of all, failure in the place of prayer. When a person prays, the life of God and the love of God fill his heart, and overflow in his life and into his words. The one who prays, flows with the gospel of the Lord, and the gospel flowing through that one leaves positive impact on others.

Nairobi, 09/06/07

177
PRAYER AND LEADERSHIP

*I*t is the responsibility of the leaders of the local church to fast and pray until everyone who is present on Sunday morning becomes a true member, who is increasingly present at the prayer meetings of the local church.

Yaounde, 12/06/07

178
PRAYER AND CHURCH MEMBERSHIP

The true members of a local church are known at the place of prayer. Those who come on Sunday morning, and do not come to any other meeting are not members, but visitors.

Yaounde, 12/06/07

179

THANKING THE LORD GOD ALMIGHTY IN EVERY CIRCUMSTANCE

Give thanks in all circumstances (1 Thessalonians 5:18).

Jos, 16/06/07,
51st missionary journey to Nigeria,
The 3rd Supra-long fast

180
DEVOTION TO THANKSGIVING

I have been commanded to devote myself to being thankful. *Devote yourselves to prayer, being watchful and thankful* (Colossians 4:2).

Jos, 16/06/07,
51st missionary journey to Nigeria,
The 3rd Supra-long fast

181
PRAYER

It is important that a person seeks and knows the will of God before he or she begins to wrestle at praying it through.

Jos, 16/06/07,
51st missionary journey to Nigeria,
The 3rd Supra-long fast

182
PRAYER

It is important that the believer seek God's will, know it, and pray it through.

Jos, 16/06/07,
51st missionary journey to Nigeria,
The 3rd Supra-long fast

HOW TO SUCCEED IN THE CHRISTIAN LIFE

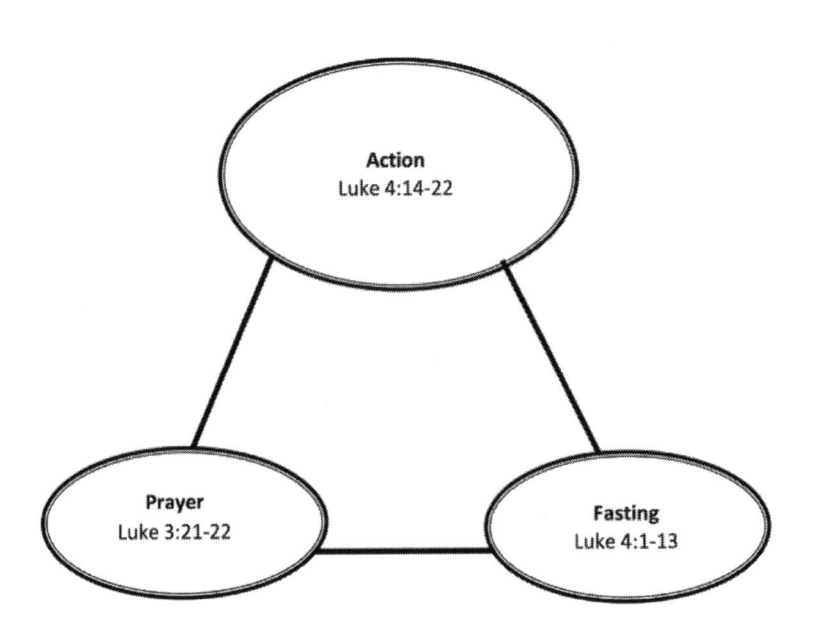

- **Action** — Luke 4:14-22
- **Prayer** — Luke 3:21-22
- **Fasting** — Luke 4:1-13

Montreal, 24/06/07

184
PRAYER AND HOLINESS

*I*t takes only one sin committed deliberately, and not confessed deeply and abandoned permanently, for true prayer to cease and meaningless noise to replace it.

Hanover, 01/07/07

185
PRAYER AND HOLINESS

There is a sense in which the extent to which a person's prayers are answered by God is directly proportional to the holiness of his life.

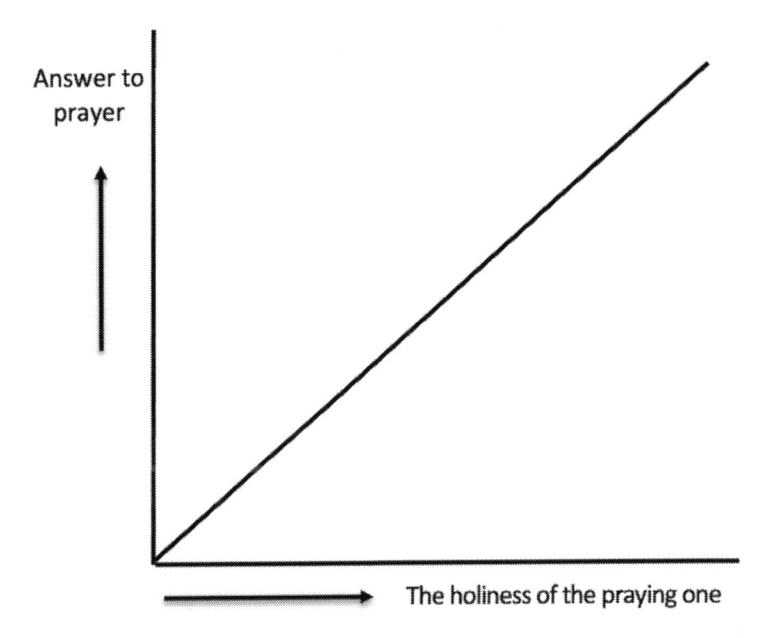

Answer to prayer ↑

→ The holiness of the praying one

Hanover, 01/07/07

PRAYER

Until I have put in my all, I should not expect God to step in. When I have put in my all, I can call on God to intervene. When I have put in my all, I can pray with expectation.

Yaounde, 07/07/07

187
PRAYER

*P*rayer must flow from a holy heart, and flow out through holy lips.

Yaounde, 12/07/07

188
PRAYER

It is a life that prays. From a life that prays, words of prayer flow out and move God to answer.

Yaounde, 12/07/07

189
PRAYER AND HOLINESS

Before a person prays about anything, he must ensure that the Holy Spirit, the resident Intercessor and the Lord Jesus Christ, the Enthroned Intercessor are praying with him to the Father, that, that thing he wants to ask for be given to him. If the Holy Spirit and the Lord Jesus are not in agreement that God should give a person a thing, God will not give the thing prayed for, regardless of how much praying is invested into it and regardless of the insistence and the persistence.

Yaounde, 13/07/07

190
PRAYER AND HOLINESS

Before a person prays, he must examine himself before the Lord, to see if there is anything in his life that will block his prayers from reaching God.

Yaounde, 13/07/07

191
PRAYER AND HOLINESS

Unless a person can say to God, "You know my heart is pure but if there is a sin hidden somewhere in my heart, show it to me and I will do all I can to immediately confess and forsake it," he prays in vain. The God of holiness cannot answer prayers that flow from a heart that keeps even one sin knowingly.

Yaounde, 17/07/07

192
PRAYER AND HOLINESS

If a man's heart is impure, he has no life of prayer, because prayer must flow from a pure heart to the God of holiness.

Yaounde, 17/07/07

193
SOUL-WINNING

A successful soul-winner will ensure that he prays three times as much as he preaches, to ensure that hearts that are either like the path, rocky places or thorny soil are transformed into good soil before the word is sown in them.

Yaounde, 22/07/07

194
SOUL-WINNING

The soul-winning that produces abiding fruits is preceded by investments in fasting and prayer, so that people whose hearts are like the path, rocky places, and thorny soil are transformed into the good soil before the seed is sown in them.

Yaounde, 22/07/07

195
PRAYER

Unless we ask the Lord, the Holy Spirit will not do any of His works in us. All the attributes of the Holy Spirit can come to us if we ask for them. He will give the Holy Spirit to those who ask Him.

Spurgeon,
Yaounde, 10/08/07

196
LEADERSHIP AND PRAYER

Progress in growth in numbers in a leader's ministry is directly proportional to the leader's progress in the prayer life.

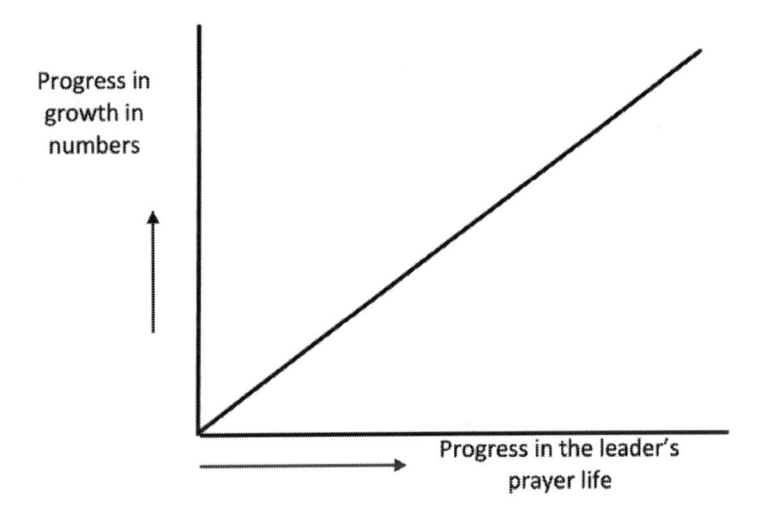

Progress in growth in numbers ↑

Progress in the leader's prayer life →

Abidjan, 25/08/07

197

LEADERSHIP AND PRAYER

*G*rowth in depth in the knowledge of the Lord Jesus Christ of the people led by a leader is directly proportional to their leader's prayer for their growth in the knowledge of the Lord.

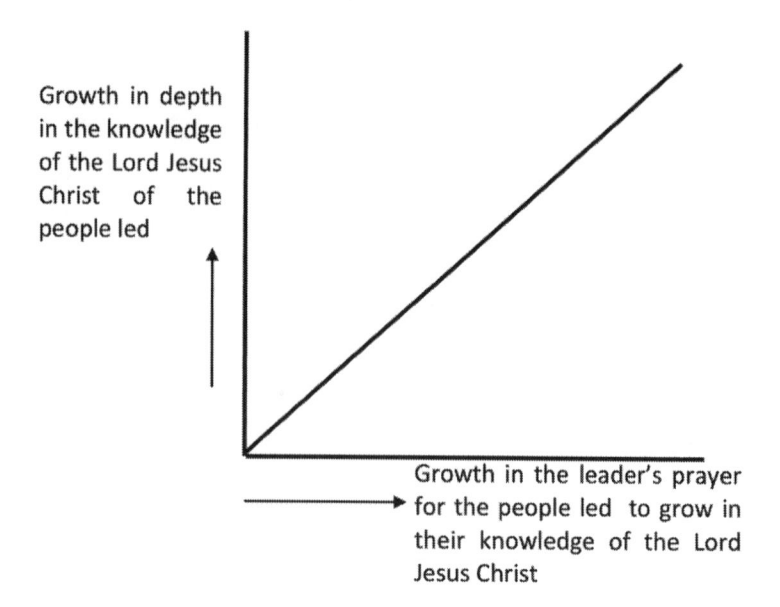

Growth in depth in the knowledge of the Lord Jesus Christ of the people led

Growth in the leader's prayer for the people led to grow in their knowledge of the Lord Jesus Christ

Abidjan, 25/08/07

198
PRAYER AND WORK FOR GOD

Any work for God that does not flow from prayer is great evil. By prayer, we mean great praying, aggressive praying, unceasing praying, forceful praying, and persistent praying.

Yaounde, 30/08/07

199
PRAYER AND WORK FOR GOD

Work for God that flows from absence of prayer, little praying or weak praying is no work. It is worse than doing nothing for God. For example, preaching that does not flow from a prayer life that satisfies the heart of God will release weak words that will inoculate people against true conviction and true conversion.

Yaounde, 30/08/07

PRAYER AND INTIMACY WITH THE ALMIGHTY

Those who are not intimate with God know their own needs and the needs of the people with whom they rub shoulders. Consequently, their prayers are filled with their needs and with those of their fellow human beings. Those who draw close to God plug into Him, and stay plugged in Him, and out of that intimacy, they get to know God's needs and so can pray them through.

Bujumbura, 01/09/07

201
PRAYER

There are three levels of prayer that correspond to a praying person's status—whether the person is a baby, a youth, or an adult. The spiritual baby is caught up with personal needs; the spiritual youth is carried away with the needs of people (others), and the spiritual adult is caught up with the needs of God.

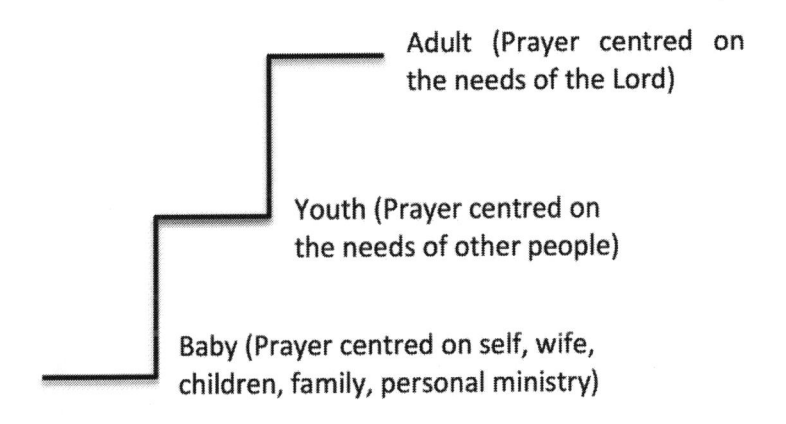

- Adult (Prayer centred on the needs of the Lord)
- Youth (Prayer centred on the needs of other people)
- Baby (Prayer centred on self, wife, children, family, personal ministry)

Bujumbura, 01/09/07

202
WORLD UNIVERSITY OF PRAYER

The World University of Prayer will produce missionaries of prayer, teachers of prayer and men and women of prayer, and labour to raise the level of the church worldwide.

Abogelbad - Egypt, 07/09/07

203
THE HOW OF PRAYER

Prayer is what is said, and how it is said.

The Lord Jesus prayed with loud cries and tears (Hebrews 5:7).

He was heard not only for what He said, but for how He said it. He is the model. Those who want God to answer their prayer should like Him pray with loud cries and tears. To fail to imitate Him in praying like Him is to fail totally.

Santa Cruz, 19/09/07

204
PRAYER

It is imperative that people be taught to pray.

The twelve saw Jesus praying, but could not simply pray because they saw Him praying. They needed to be taught to pray and they asked to be taught. Each one needs to be taught to pray. Everyone needs a teacher to lead him or her to pray.

Abogelbad – Egypt, 07/09/07

205

THE HOW OF PRAYER

The one who prays does so in eager expectation of the answer. When Elijah began to pray, he asked his servant from time to time to look and see if the answer had been sent. **1Kgs ...** *But Elijah climbed to the top of Carmel, bent down to the ground and put his face between his knees. Go and look toward the sea, he told his servant. And he went up and looked.*

"There is nothing there,"

he said. Seven times Elijah said,

"Go back."

The seventh time the servant reported,

"A cloud as small as a man's hand is rising from the sea."

So Elijah said,

> "Go and tell Ahab, 'Hitch up your chariot and go down before the rain stops you' " (*1 kings 18: 42-44*).

He expected God to answer imminently and so pressed home his request in total self-pouring and great expectation. Those who pray should expect God to answer without delay. He will answer you without delay; Pray! Pray!! Pray!!!

Santa Cruz, 19/09/07

206
PRAYER

Prayer flows from the heart of God to the heart of man and back to the heart of God. When God wants to do a thing, He lays the burden in His heart on the heart of someone who prays. That person will begin to transform that burden into prayer, and this way God will be moved to do that which He wants.

Yaounde, 29/09/07

207
HOW TO PRAY

*I*f one wants to pray, it will help if one takes a paper and a pen before the Lord and writes down each aspect of the issues to be raised to God in prayer. After writing down the aspects that immediately come to his or her heart, he or she can ask the Lord to reveal other aspects about the issue, and as the Lord reveals these, he or she should add them to the list of what is to be asked in prayer. When this is done, the reception of what to pray about is complete. This is then followed by lifting to the Lord silently or violently, each of the aspects written down. This asking can be carried out with words known, with words unknown or without words.

Yaounde, 29/09/07

208

PRAYER AND BURDEN

Prayer is the overflow of burden. No burden, no prayer. Little burden, little prayer, much burden, much prayer. Extreme burden, extreme prayer. We can say that prayer is directly proportional to the burden of the praying one.

Prayer

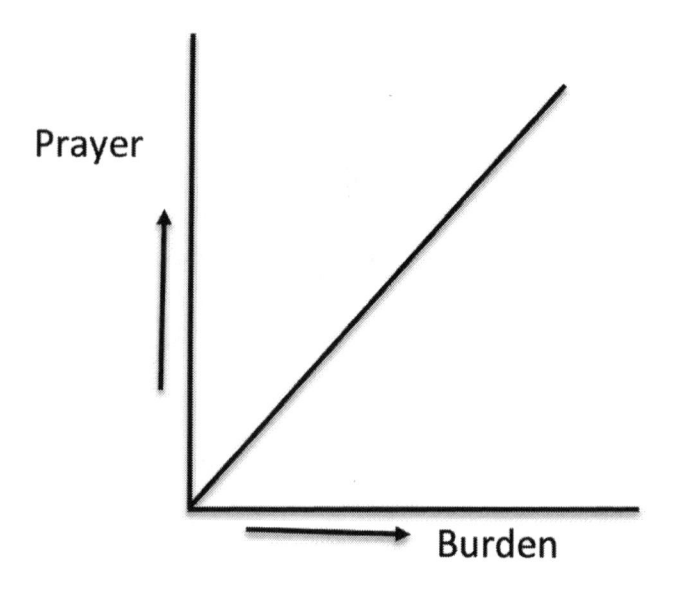

Burden

Stockholm, 10/10/07

209
ANSWERS TO PRAYER AND BURDEN

A person does not only pray according to his burden. He receives answers from God according to his burden because those without burden will pray carelessly and stop. They will also receive no answers from God. Those with some burden will pray more and they may receive some answers from God. Those with crushing burdens will pray desperately and they will surely be heard by God and their requests granted. So we can say that answers to prayer are directly proportional to burden.

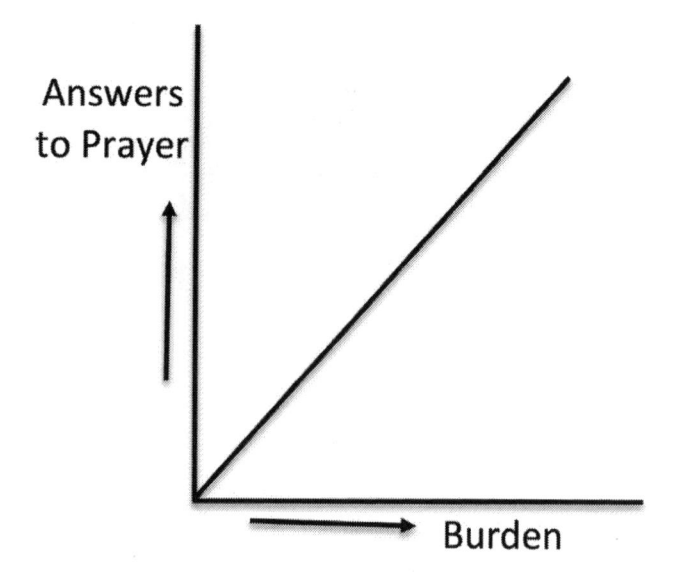

Stockholm, 10/10/07

210
PRAYER

Through prayer, hopeless situation are relieved. Prayerlessness is cooperation with the devil. Little praying is cooperation with the devil. Weak praying is cooperation with the devil. When God is brought in through prayer, He dismantles the devil's plans and projects and ousts him from the situation. Everyone who wants to succeed must bring God into the situation through prayer alone, and prayer with others.

Yaounde, 27/10/07,
1st missionary journey to Bata,
6th missionary journey to Equatorial Guinea

211
PRAYER

Prayer transforms a weak person into a strong person; it transforms a lazy person into a hard-working person, transforms short-sighted people into people who see far and transforms confused people into people who are settled and goal-directed. Prayer transforms churches with a few members into churches with large numbers. Prayer transforms churches where people come and go, into churches in which people come, stay, and become useful members.

Bata, 27/10/07,
1st missionary journey to Bata,
6th missionary journey to Equatorial Guinea

PRAYER AND SPIRITUAL LEADERSHIP

Spiritual leadership is the call to build the kingdom of the Lord Jesus Christ and to destroy the Kingdom of Satan. The Kingdom of the Lord is built and the kingdom of Satan destroyed in the place of prayer. The devil is most active from 7 p.m. to 5 a.m. Those who want to destroy his kingdom are at work from 7 p.m. to 5 a.m. praying. If there is no one to pray against Satan at these hours, a leader is lacking in that city or locality and Satan will continue to hold sway.

Guinea Bissau, 03/11/07,
2nd missionary journey to Guinea Bissau

213
PRAYER

The devil is a ruthless destroyer. He works to destroy. He is like resting in the day in order to fully attack at night. He starts at 7 p.m. and continues to 5 a.m. Those who must destroy the devil must attack him by praying against him during those hours. If a warrior has a church of 14 members and wants to take a city for the Lord Jesus, he will position two of those members to pray from 7 p.m. to 5 a.m. on Mondays; two other members to pray from 7 p.m. to 5 a.m. on Tuesdays; and so forth. With the devil opposed at the place of prayer seven days a week, his plans will fail and those of the Lord will succeed.

Guinea Bissau, 03/11/07

214
PRAYER

*P*rayer is calling upon the Lord to destroy the hosts of hell and their activities. The more praying at night there is, the more the devil is hindered. The less praying there is, the less the enemy is hindered. This is because the devil does his worst when he is unhindered. The devil had wanted to strike Job, but he was hindered by the barrier that God had put.

> *Have you not put a hedge around him and his household and everything he has? You have blessed the work of his hands, so that his flocks and herds are spread throughout the land* (Job 1:10).

Bissau, 03/11/07

215
PRAYER

When a prayer night where two or more people pray for eight to ten hours one night a week exists in a locality, the church truly exists in that locality. Where there is no prayer night, the church is yet to be born in that locality. The devil does his work mainly at night, and when the church prays at night, she stands in the way of the devil in a way that prayer in the day cannot stand.

Bissau, 03/11/07

216
PRAYER

Expecting God to do great things without there being heavy praying and heavy fasting to move Him to release the great things from Heaven is false expectation.

Yaounde, 28/11/07

217
PRAYER

God has promised me great, very great, sensational, fantastic and awesome things. If I pray, God will fulfil His promise and the great, very great, sensational, fantastic and awesome things that He has promised will come to pass. If I do not pray, if I pray little or if I pray lightly, the great, sensational, fantastic and awesome things that He has promised will not happen.

Yaounde, 28/11/07,
Concluding the special missionary journey to Jerusalem

218
PRAYER

"Lord, difficulties compel me to cry out to You. Lord send me ever-increasing difficulties so that I may cling unceasingly to You."

*A*postle Paul wrote, *To keep me from becoming conceited because of these surpassingly great revelations, there was given me a thorn in my flesh, a messenger of Satan, to torment me. Three times I pleaded with the Lord to take it away from me. But he said to me,*

> *"My grace is sufficient for you, for my power is made perfect in weakness." Therefore I will boast all the more gladly about my weaknesses, so that Christ's power may rest on me. That is why, for Christ's sake, I delight in weaknesses, in insults, in hardships, in persecutions, in difficulties. For when I am weak, then I am strong* (2 Corinthians 12:7–10).

Hardships, difficulties, calamities move all believers to pray. Lord, may my life never be easy so that I would never slacken in prayer.

Jerusalem, 02/12/07

219
PRAYER

What is asked for in prayer is directly proportional to the knowledge of God of the person who asks. Those who do not know God ask vaguely, lightheartedly and faintly. Those who know God ask specifically, wholeheartedly and boldly, because they know that they will surely receive what they are asking.

Jerusalem, 03/12/07

220
PRAYER

What a person asks for in prayer reflects the person's faith in God. If the person's faith in God is great the person will ask for the near impossible, because the person believes that nothing is impossible with God. So we can say that a person asks in direct proportion to his faith. No faith, no asking; little faith, little asking, great faith, great asking.

PRAYER

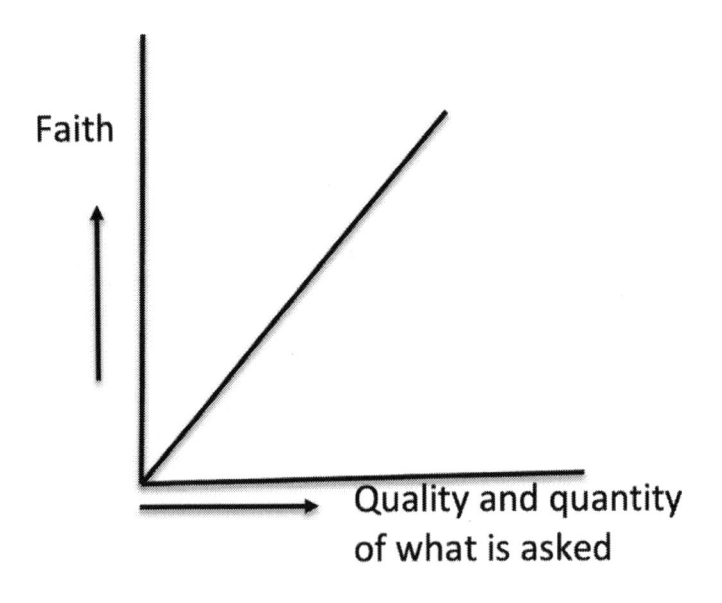

Faith ↑

→ Quality and quantity of what is asked

Jerusalem, 03/12/07

221
PRAYING IN THE NAME OF THE LORD JESUS

To pray in the name of the Lord Jesus is to pray for what the Lord Jesus is praying for. To pray for it in the way He is praying for it from the throne, and to pray for it from a heart and life that are absolutely surrendered, entirely sanctified, filled to overflowing with the Holy Spirit, absolutely consecrated, entirely consecrated to the Lord Jesus and the gospel, and perfected. It must be prayed so that the Lord Jesus and He alone should receive the glory for the answer when it is sent down from heaven.

Between Johannesburg and Australia, 10/12/07

222
PRAYING IN THE NAME OF THE LORD JESUS

For prayer to be made in the name of the Lord Jesus Christ, the one who prays must be as perfect as his Father who is in Heaven is. He must pray what the Lord Jesus is praying; he must ask with the motives that the Lord Jesus is asking; he must ask with all his spirit, all his soul and with all his might, as the Lord Jesus Christ prays, and he must insist as the Lord Jesus is insisting. He must also pray in the power of the Holy Spirit as the Lord Jesus does pray, so that God alone would answer, and pray so that all glory for the answers received will be given to the Lord Jesus and Him alone.

Between Johannesburg and Australia, 10/12/07

223
PRAYER

The Holy Spirit wanted to come down on the Lord Jesus, but He was blocked by the sealed heavens. The Lord Jesus tore the heavens open by His prayers and as soon as the heavens were torn open, the Holy Spirit came upon Him.

> *As Jesus was coming up out of the water, <u>he saw heaven being torn open</u> and the Spirit descending on him like a dove* (Mark 1: 10).

When all the people were being baptized, Jesus was baptized too. And as he was praying, heaven was opened and the Holy Spirit descended on him in bodily form like a dove. And a voice came from heaven:

> *"You are my Son, whom I love; with you I am well pleased"* (Luke 3:21-22).

The Hague, 02/02/08

224
PRAYER

That the Lord Jesus lives evermore to intercede, that He interceded on earth and has been interceding since His return to the Throne compels me to conclude that there are two absolute musts in prayer—the quality and the quantity. The Lord has always prayed quality prayers but we find that He is offering quality prayer increasingly. Unless my life is one of unceasing quality prayer, I will fail to prevail.

> "O Lord, help me to offer quality prayers unceasingly so that Your work in my life and through my life may succeed. Lord, help me to offer to You perfect prayers in ceaseless abundance."
>
> ***The Hague, 02/02/08***

225
PRAYER

The Bible says,

Therefore he is able to save completely those who come to God through him, because he always lives to intercede for them (Hebrews 7:25).

The Lord Jesus Christ has already prayed for 1973 × 365 × 24 = 17,283,480 hours as at this date. The Son of God understands that quality in prayer is absolutely indispensable. The Son on the Throne is praying unceasingly that the church should be without spot, without wrinkle and without blemish. He is praying that the church may become a glorious church. If the praying already invested is not yet enough for the Father to answer, then the reason for so many unanswered prayers is that so little praying has been invested.

Yaounde, 05/02/08

226
PRAYER

It is deeply troubling what depends on man. It is possible to have entire villages, towns, regions and continents believe in the Lord Jesus Christ if enough prayers are invested in the project. God wants to do it, but He has decided that He will not do it unless He receives quality and quantity praying.

Yaounde, 05/02/08

227
VIOLENCE IN PRAYER

During the days of Jesus' life on earth he offered up prayers and petitions with loud cries and tears to the one who could save him from death, and he was heard because of his reverent submission (Hebrews 5:7).

The Lord Jesus prayed with loud cries and tears and was heard. Had He prayed with indulgent ease, He would not have been heard. He prayed violently. Nonviolent praying is not praying at all. God will not hear nonviolent prayers.

Libreville, 18/02/08

228
PRAYER

The Lord is able to save to the uttermost because He lives evermore to intercede. The extent to which He is able to save is directly proportional to the extent to which He prays.

but because Jesus lives forever, he has a permanent priesthood.

> Therefore he is able to save completely those who come to God through him, because he always lives to intercede for them (Hebrews 7:24-25).

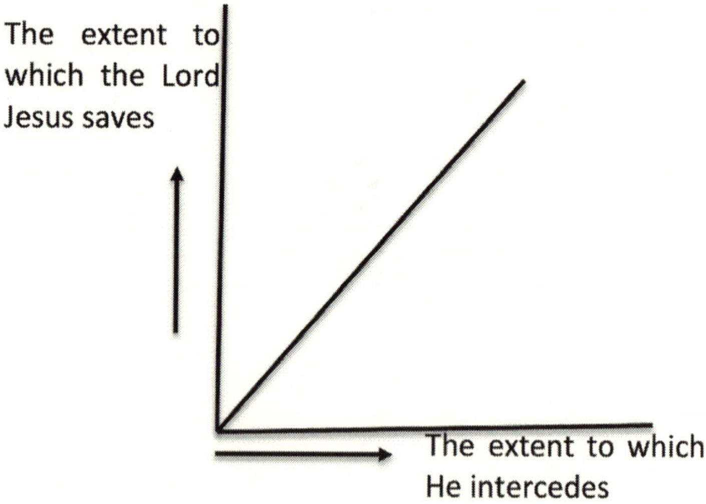
The extent to which the Lord Jesus saves
The extent to which He intercedes

Libreville, 18/02/08

229
INTENSITY IN PRAYER

The Lord Jesus prayed with such sustained intensity that His blood vessels broke and His sweat became drops of blood falling to the ground.

And being in anguish, he prayed more earnestly, and his sweat was like drops of blood falling to the ground (Luke 22:44).

Libreville, 18/02/08

230
INTENSITY IN PRAYER

The Lord Jesus prayed so intensely that it became necessary for the Father to send an angel from heaven to strengthen Him.

An angel from heaven appeared to him and strengthened him (Luke 22:43).

He prayed to near total exhaustion, so that he needed strengthening by an angel.

Libreville, 18/02/08

231
PRAYER

*P*raying in the name of the Lord is <u>praying as the Lord Jesus Christ prayed and is praying.</u> He prayed with loud cries and tears,

> *During the days of Jesus' life on earth, he offered up prayers and petitions with loud cries and tears to the one who could save him from death, and he was heard because of his reverent submission* (Hebrews 5:7).

He prayed until his sweat was like drops of blood falling to the ground. *And being in anguish, he prayed more earnestly, and his sweat was like drops of blood falling to the ground* (Luke 22:44).

Yaounde, 19/02/08

232
PRAYER

Praying in the name of the Lord Jesus Christ is praying <u>for the things that the Lord Jesus Christ is praying for from the Throne.</u>

Yaounde, 19/02/08

BACK MATTERS

THANK YOU
For Reading This Book

If you have any question and/or need help, do not hesitate to contact us through **ztfbooks@cmfionline.org**. If the book has blessed you, then we would also be grateful if you leave a positive review at your favorite retailer.

ZTF BOOKS, through Christian Publishing House (CPH) offers a wide selection of best selling Christian books (in print, eBook & audiobook formats) on a broad spectrum of topics, including marriage & family, sexuality, practical spiritual warfare, Christian service, Christian leadership, and much more. Visit us at **ztfbooks.com** to learn more about our latest releases and special offers. And thank you for being a ZTF BOOK reader.

We invite you to connect with more from the author through social media (**cmfionline**) and/or ministry website (**ztfministry.org**), where we offer both on-ground and remote training courses (all year round) from basic to university level at the University of Prayer and Fasting (WUPF) and the School of Knowing and Serving God (SKSG). You are highly welcome to enrol at your soonest convenience. A FREE online Bible Course is also available.

Finally, we would like to recommend to you the next suitable book, *The Way Of Christian Character*:

This book is about the character of Christ that the believer is called to put on. Christlike character formation in us is the work of the Holy Spirit who dwells in us.

In this book, you will find well-developed, rich definitions and sound concepts surrounding the notion of the character of Christ. Themes that have been properly developed include

- the origin of worldly character,
- the dangers of worldly character,
- Christian character, and
- how Christian character is acquired.

As you read this book, you will discover that spirituality is not measured according to spiritual gifts but, rather, by the character of Christ manifested through our body in which the death of Christ manifests.

This is a book to be classified among rare masterpieces which can lead the believer to experience the sanctified life in an ever-increasing way.

It's a book to read in prayer with eternity in view.

It's highly recommended.

THANK YOU

For Reading This Book

If you have any question and/or need help, do not hesitate to contact us through **ztfbooks@cmfionline.org**. If the book has blessed you, then we would also be grateful if you leave a positive review at your favorite retailer.

ZTF BOOKS, through Christian Publishing House (CPH) offers a wide selection of best selling Christian books (in print, eBook & audiobook formats) on a broad spectrum of topics, including marriage & family, sexuality, practical spiritual warfare, Christian service, Christian leadership, and much more. Visit us at **ztfbooks.com** to learn more about our latest releases and special offers. And thank you for being a ZTF BOOK reader.

We invite you to connect with more from the author through social media (**cmfionline**) and/or ministry website (**ztfministry.org**), where we offer both on-ground and remote training courses (all year round) from basic to university level at the University of Prayer and Fasting (WUPF) and the School of Knowing and Serving God (SKSG). You are highly welcome to enrol at your soonest convenience. A FREE online Bible Course is also available.

Finally, we would like to recommend to you the next suitable book, _Learning to Importune in Prayer_:

The Holy art of importunate praying and intercession.

Importunity, says *Prof. Fomum*, is the cry of a man in extreme danger. It is madly asking God to open a door through the wall of a situation - until the door is opened. Importunity has God's interest in view; it is taking no rest until God is moved to do that which He alone must do. He affirms that <u>when God gives you a number of problems to which man has no answers, then He has promoted you - He has given you materials for importunity praying.</u>

God's purposes in the New Covenant are tied to the Spirit-filled life. Christian service also starts with this quality of life. He reiterates his heart's cry to see the leader strive to be Spirit-filled and press on to attain to the fullness of the Holy Spirit.

We send out this book with prayer that the Lord would use it to produce men and women of importunate praying—watchmen at the gates of Jerusalem.

VERY IMPORTANT!!!

If you have not yet received Jesus as your Lord and Saviour, I encourage you to receive Him. Here are some steps to help you,

ADMIT that you are a sinner by nature and by practice and that on your own you are without hope. Tell God you have personally sinned against Him in your thoughts, words and deeds. Confess your sins to Him, one after another in a sincere prayer. Do not leave out any sins that you can remember. Truly turn from your sinful ways and abandon them. If you stole, steal no more. If you have been committing adultery or fornication, stop it. God will not forgive you if you have no desire to stop sinning in all areas of your life, but if you are sincere, He will give you the power to stop sinning.

BELIEVE that Jesus Christ, who is God's Son, is the only Way, the only Truth and the only Life. Jesus said,

> "I am the way, the truth and the life; no one comes to the Father, but by me" (John 14:6).

The Bible says,

> "For there is one God, and there is one mediator between God and men, the man Christ Jesus, who gave himself as a ransom for all" (1 Timothy 2:5-6).

> "And there is salvation in no one else (apart from Jesus), for there is no other name under heaven given among men by which we must be saved" (Acts 4:12).

> But to all who received him, who believed in his name, he gave power to become children of God..." (John 1:12).

BUT,

CONSIDER the cost of following Him. Jesus said that all who follow Him must deny themselves, and this includes selfish financial, social and other interests. He also wants His followers to take up their crosses and follow Him. Are you prepared to abandon your own interests daily for those of Christ? Are you prepared to be led in a new direction by Him? Are you prepared to suffer for Him and die for Him if need be? Jesus will have nothing to do with half-hearted people. His demands are total. He will only receive and forgive those who are prepared to follow Him AT ANY COST. Think about it and count the cost. If you are prepared to follow Him, come what may, then there is something to do.

INVITE Jesus to come into your heart and life. He says,

> "Behold I stand at the door and knock. If anyone hears my voice and opens the door (to his heart and life), I will come in to him and eat with him, and he with me " (Revelation 3:20).

VERY IMPORTANT!!!

Why don't you pray a prayer like the following one or one of your own construction as the Holy Spirit leads?

> *"Lord Jesus, I am a wretched, lost sinner who has sinned in thought, word and deed. Forgive all my sins and cleanse me. Receive me, Saviour and transform me into a child of God. Come into my heart now and give me eternal life right now. I will follow you at all costs, trusting the Holy Spirit to give me all the power I need."*

When you pray this prayer sincerely, Jesus answers at once and justifies you before God and makes you His child.

> *Please write to us (**ztfbooks@cmfionline.org**) and I will pray for you and help you as you go on with Jesus Christ.*

ABOUT THE AUTHOR

Professor Zacharias Tanee Fomum was born in the flesh on 20th June 1945 and became born again on 13th June 1956. On 1st October 1966, He consecrated his life to the Lord Jesus and to His service, and was filled with the Holy Spirit on 24th October 1970. He was taken to be with the Lord on 14th March, 2009.

Pr Fomum was admitted to a first class in the Bachelor of Science degree, graduating as a prize winning student from Fourah Bay College in the University of Sierra Leone in October 1969. At the age of 28, he was awarded a Ph.D. in Organic Chemistry by the University of Makerere, Kampala in Uganda. In October 2005, he was awarded a Doctor of Science (D.Sc) by the University of Durham, Great Britain. This higher doctorate was in recognition of his distinct contributions to scientific knowledge through research. As a Professor of Organic Chemistry in the University of Yaoundé 1, Cameroon, Professor Fomum supervised or co-supervised more than 100 Master's Degree and Doctoral Degree theses and co-authored over 160 scientific articles in leading international journals. He considered Jesus Christ the Lord of Science ("For by Him all things were created..." – Colossians 1:16), and scientific research an act of obedience to God's command to "subdue the earth" (Genesis 1:28). He therefore made the Lord Jesus the Director of his research laboratory while he took the place of deputy director, and attributed his outstanding success as a scientist to Jesus' revelational leadership.

In more than 40 years of Christian ministry, Pr Fomum travelled extensively, preaching the Gospel, planting churches and training spiritual leaders. He made more than:

- 700 missionary journeys within Cameroon, which ranged from one day to three weeks in duration.
- 500 missionary journeys to more than 70 different nations in all the six continents. These ranged from two days to six weeks in duration.

By the time of his going to be with the Lord in 2009, he had preached in over 1000 localities in Cameroon, sent over 200 national missionaries into many localities in Cameroon and planted over 1300 churches in the various administrative provinces of Cameroon. At his base in Yaoundé, he planted and built a mega-church with his co-workers which grew to a steady membership of about 12,000. Pr Fomum was the founding team-leader of Christian Missionary Fellowship International (CMFI); an evangelism, soul-winning, disciple making, Church-planting and missionary-sending movement with more than 200 international missionaries and thousands of churches in 65 nations spread across Africa, Europe, the Americas, Asia and Oceania. In the course of their ministry, Pr Fomum and his team witnessed more than 10,000 recorded healing miracles performed by God in answer to prayer in the name of Jesus Christ. These miracles include instant healings of headaches, cancers, HIV/AIDS, blindness, deafness, dumbness, paralysis, madness, and new teeth and organs received.

Pr Fomum read the entire Bible more than 60 times, read more than 1350 books on the Christian faith and authored over 150 books to advance the Gospel of Jesus Christ. 5 million copies of these books are in circulation in 12 languages as well as 16 million gospel tracts in 17 languages.

Pr Fomum was a man who sought God. He spent between 15 minutes and six hours daily alone with God in what he called Daily Dynamic Encounters with God (DDEWG). During these DDEWG he read God's Word, meditated on it, listened to God's voice, heard God speak to him, recorded what God was saying to him and prayed it through. He thus had over 18,000 DDEWG. He also had over 60 periods of withdrawing to seek God alone for periods that ranged from 3 to 21 days (which he termed Retreats for Spiritual Progress). The time he spent seeking God slowly transformed him into a man who hungered, thirsted and panted after God. His unceasing heart cry was: "Oh, that I would have more of God!"

Pr Fomum was a man of prayer and a leading teacher on prayer in many churches and conferences around the world. He considered prayer to be the most important work that can be done for God and for man. He was a man of faith who believed that God answers prayer. He kept a record of his prayer requests and had over 50, 000 recorded answers to prayer in his prayer books. He carried out over 100 Prayer Walks of between five and forty-seven kilometres in towns and cities around the world. He and his team carried out over 57 Prayer Crusades (periods of forty days and nights during which at least eight hours are invested into prayer each day). They also carried out over 80 Prayer Sieges (times of near non-stop praying that ranges from 24 hours to 120 hours). He authored the Prayer Power Series, a 13-volume set of books on various aspects of prayer; Supplication, Fasting, Intercession and Spiritual Warfare. He started prayer chains, prayer rooms, prayer houses, national and continental prayer movements in Cameroon and other nations. He worked with leaders of local churches in India to disciple and train more than 2 million believers.

Pr Fomum also considered fasting as one of the weapons of Christian Spiritual Warfare. He carried out over 250 fasts ranging from three days to forty days, drinking only water or water supplemented with soluble vitamins. Called by the Lord to a distinct ministry of intercession, he pioneered fasting and prayer movements and led in battles against principalities and powers obstructing the progress of the Gospel and God's global purposes. He was enabled to carry out 3 supra – long fasts of between 52 and 70 days in his final years.

Pr Fomum chose a lifestyle of simplicity and "self- imposed poverty" in order to invest more funds into the critical work of evangelism, soul winning, church-planting and the building up of believers. Knowing the importance of money and its role in the battle to reach those without Christ with the glorious Gospel, he and his wife grew to investing 92.5% of their earned income from all sources (salaries, allowances, royalties and cash gifts) into the Gospel. They invested with the hope that, as they grew in the knowledge and the love of the Lord, and the perishing souls of people, they would one day invest 99% of their income into the Gospel.

He was married to Prisca Zei Fomum and they had seven children who are all involved in the work of the Gospel, some serving as missionaries. Prisca is a national and international minister, specializing in the winning and discipling of children to Jesus Christ. She also communicates and imparts the vision of ministry to children with a view to raising and building up ministers to them.

The Professor owed all that he was and all that God had done through him, to the unmerited favour and blessing of God and to his worldwide army of friends and co-workers. He considered himself nothing without them and the blessing of God; and would have amounted to nothing but for them. All praise and glory to Jesus Christ!

- facebook.com/cmfionline
- twitter.com/cmfionline
- instagram.com/cmfionline
- pinterest.com/cmfionline
- youtube.com/cmfionline

ALSO BY Z.T. FOMUM

https://ztfbooks.com

THE CHRISTIAN WAY

1. The Way Of Life
2. The Way Of Obedience
3. The Way Of Discipleship
4. The Way Of Sanctification
5. The Way Of Christian Character
6. The Way Of Spiritual Power
7. The Way Of Christian Service
8. The Way Of Spiritual Warfare
9. The Way Of Suffering For Christ
10. The Way Of Victorious Praying
11. The Way Of Overcomers
12. The Way Of Spiritual Encouragement
13. The Way Of Loving The Lord

THE PRAYER POWER SERIES

1. The Way Of Victorious Praying
2. The Ministry Of Fasting
3. The Art Of Intercession
4. The Practice Of Intercession
5. Praying With Power
6. Practical Spiritual Warfare Through Prayer
7. Moving God Through Prayer
8. The Ministry Of Praise And Thanksgiving
9. Waiting On The Lord In Prayer

10. The Ministry Of Supplication
11. Life-Changing Thoughts On Prayer (Vol. 1)
12. The Centrality of Prayer
13. Life-Changing Thoughts On Prayer (Vol. 2)
14. Life-Changing Thoughts on Prayer (Vol. 3)
15. The Art of Worship
16. Life-Changing Thoughts on Prayer (Vol. 4)
17. Life-Changing Thoughts on Prayer (Vol. 5)
18. Learning to Importune in Prayer
19. Prayer And A Walk With God
20. From His Prayer files
21. Prayer and Holiness
22. Practical Helps in Fasting Long Fasts
23. Life-Changing Thoughts on Fasting (Vol 1)
24. Life-Changing Thoughts on Fasting (Vol 2)

PRACTICAL HELPS FOR OVERCOMERS

1. Discipleship at any cost
2. The Use Of Time
3. Retreats For Spiritual Progress
4. Personal Spiritual Revival
5. Daily Dynamic Encounters With God
6. The School Of Truth
7. How To Succeed In The Christian Life
8. The Christian And Money
9. Deliverance From The Sin Of Laziness
10. The Art Of Working Hard
11. Knowing God - The Greatest Need Of The Hour
12. Restitution - An Important Message For The Overcomers
13. Revelation: A Must
14. The Overcomer As A Servant Of Man

15. True Repentance
16. You Can Receive A Pure Heart Today
17. You Can Lead Someone To The Lord Jesus Today
18. You Can Receive The Baptism Into The Holy Spirit Now
19. The Dignity Of Manual Labour
20. You Have A Talent!
21. The Making Of Disciples
22. The Secret Of Spiritual Fruitfulness
23. Are You Still A Disciple Of The Lord Jesus?
24. Who Is Truly a Disciple of The Lord Jesus?

LEADING GOD'S PEOPLE

1. Vision, Burden, Action
2. Knowing The God Of Unparalleled Goodness
3. Brokenness: The Secret Of Spiritual Overflow
4. The Secret Of Spiritual Rest
5. Spiritual Aggressiveness
6. The Character And The Personality of The Leader
7. Leading A Local Church
8. The Leader And His God
9. Revolutionary Thoughts On Spiritual Leadership
10. Leading God's People
11. Laws Of Spiritual Leadership
12. Laws Of Spiritual Success, Volume 1
13. The Shepherd And The Flock
14. Basic Christian Leadership
15. A Missionary life and a missionary heart
16. Spiritual Nobility
17. Spiritual Leadership in the Pattern of David
18. The Heart Surgery for the Potential Minister of the Gospel

19. Prerequisites For Spiritual Ministry
20. Power For Service
21. In The Crucible For Service
22. Qualifications For Serving in The Gospel
23. You, Your Team, And Your Ministry
24. Church Planting Strategies
25. Critical Ingredients for Successful Spiritual Leadership
26. The Power of a Man's All

GOD, SEX AND YOU

1. Enjoying The Premarital Life
2. Enjoying The Choice Of Your Marriage Partner
3. Enjoying The Married Life
4. Divorce And Remarriage
5. A Successful Marriage; The Husband's Making
6. A Successful Marriage; The Wife's Making
7. Life-changing Thoughts On Marriage

OFF-SERIES

1. Inner Healing
2. No Failure Needs To Be Final
3. Facing Life's Problems Victoriously
4. A Word To The Students
5. Blessings and Curses
6. Spiritual Fragrance (Volume 1)
7. Roots And Destinies
8. Walking With God (Vol. 1)
9. God Centredness
10. Victorious Dispositions
11. The Processes Of Faith

12. The Spirit-Filled Life
13. God, Money, And You
14. Knowing God And Walking With Him
15. Knowing and Serving God (Volume 2)
16. Esther
17. The Church: Rights And Responsibilities of The Believer
18. Children in God's Eternal Purposes

PRACTICAL HELPS IN SANCTIFICATION

1. Deliverance From Sin
2. The Way Of Sanctification
3. Sanctified And Consecrated For Spiritual Ministry
4. The Sower, The Seed, And The Hearts Of Men
5. Freedom From The Sin Of Adultery And Fornication
6. The Sin Before You May Lead To Immediate Death: Do Not Commit It!
7. Be Filled With The Holy Spirit
8. The Power Of The Holy Spirit In The Winning Of The Lost
9. Deliverance from the Sin of Gluttony
10. A Vessel of Honour
11. The Believer's Conscience
12. Practical Dying To Self And
13. The Spirit-filled Life
14. Issues of The Heart
15. Rebellion

MAKING SPIRITUAL PROGRESS

1. The Ministers And The Ministry of The New Covenant

2. The Cross In The Life And Ministry Of The Believer
3. Making Spiritual Progress, Volume 1
4. Making Spiritual Progress, Volume 2
5. Making Spiritual Progress, Volume 3
6. Making Spiritual Progress, Volume 4
7. Moving on With The Lord Jesus Christ
8. The Narrow Way (Volume 1)
9. Making Spiritual Progress (Volumes 1-4)

EVANGELISM

1. 36 Reasons For Winning The Lost To Christ
2. Soul Winning, Volume 1
3. Soul Winning, Volume 2
4. The Winning of The Lost as Life's Supreme Task
5. Salvation And Soul-Winning
6. Soul Winning And The Making Of Disciples
7. <u>Victorious Soul-Winning</u>

GOD LOVES YOU

1. God's Love And Forgiveness
2. The Way Of Life
3. Come Back Home My Son; I Still Love You
4. Jesus Loves You And Wants To Heal You
5. Come And See; Jesus Has Not Changed!
6. Celebrity A Mask
7. Encounter The Saviour
8. Meet The Liberator
9. Jesus Saves And Heals Today
10. Jesus is The Answer

WOMEN OF THE GLORY

1. **The Secluded Worshipper: Prophetess Anna**
2. **Unending Intimacy: Mary of Bethany**
3. **Winning Love: Mary Magdalene**

ZTF COMPLETE WORKS

1. The School of Soul Winners and Soul Winning
2. The Complete Works of Z.T.F on Holiness (Volume 1)
3. The Complete Works of Z.T.F on Basic Christian Doctrine
4. The Complete Works of Z.T.F on Marriage (Volume 1)
5. The Complete Works of Z.T.F on The Gospel Message (Volume 1)
6. The Complete Works of Z.T.F on Prayer (Volume 1)
7. The Complete Works of Z.T.F on Prayer (Volume 2)
8. The Complete Works of Z.T.F on Prayer (Volume 3)
9. The Complete Works of Z.T.F on Prayer (Volume 4)
10. The Complete Works of Z.T.F on Prayer (Volume 5)
11. The Complete Works of Z.T.F on Leadership (Volume 1)
12. The Complete Works of Z.T.F on Leadership (Volume 2)
13. The Complete Works of Z.T.F on Leadership (Volume 3)

SPECIAL SERIES

1. A Broken Vessel

2. The Joy of Begging to Belong to the Lord Jesus Christ: A Testimony

ZTF AUTO-BIOGRAPHIES

1. From His Lips: About The Author
2. From His Lips: About His Co-Workers
3. From His Lips: Back From His Missions
4. From His Lips: About Our Ministry
5. From His Lips: On Our Vision
6. From His Lips: The work is the worker
7. From His Lips: The Battles He Fought
8. From His Lips: The Authority And Power of His Life
9. From His Lips: The Influences That Moulded Him: People And Books

THE OVERTHROW OF PRINCIPALITIES

1. Deliverance From Demons
2. The Prophecy Of The Overthrow Of The Satanic Prince Of Cameroon
3. The Prophecy of the Overthrow of The Satanic Prince of Yaounde
4. The Prophecy of the Overthrow of The Satanic Prince of Douala
5. The overthrow of principalities and powers
6. From His Lips: The Battles He Fought

CONTINUOUS PERSONAL SPIRITUAL REVIVAL

1. Victorious Proclamations

OTHER BOOKS

1. The Missionary as a Son
2. What Our Ministry is
3. Conserver la Moisson
4. Disciples of Jesus Christ to Make Disciples For Jesus Christ
5. The House Church in God's Eternal Purposes
6. Christian Maturation
7. Heroes of the Kingdom
8. Spiritual Leadership in the Pattern of Gideon
9. The School of Evangelism
10. A Good Minister of Jesus Christ
11. Building a Spiritual Nation: The Foundation
12. Building a Spiritual Nation: Spiritual Statesmanship
13. Removing Obstacles Through Prayer and Fasting
14. The Chronicles of Our Ministry
15. The Making of Disciples: The Master's Way

DISTRIBUTORS OF ZTF BOOKS

These books can be obtained in French and English Language from any of the following distribution outlets:

EDITIONS DU LIVRE CHRETIEN (ELC)

- **Location:** Paris, France
- **Email**: editionlivrechretien@gmail.com
- **Phone:** +33 6 98 00 90 47

INTERNET

- **Location:** on all major online **eBook, Audiobook** and **print-on-demand** (paperback) retailers (Amazon, Google, iBooks, B&N, Ingram, NotionPress, etc.).
- **Email**: ztfbooks@cmfionline.org
- **Phone**: +47 454 12 804
- **Website**: ztfbooks.com

CPH YAOUNDE

- **Location:** Yaounde, Cameroon
- **Email:** editionsztf@gmail.com
- **Phone:** +237 74756559

ZTF LITERATURE AND MEDIA HOUSE

- **Location:** Lagos, Nigeria
- **Email:** zlmh@ztfministry.org
- **Phone:** +2348152163063

CPH BURUNDI

- **Location:** Bujumbura, Burundi
- **Email:** cph-burundi@ztfministry.org
- **Phone:** +257 79 97 72 75

CPH UGANDA

- **Location:** Kampala, Uganda
- **Email:** cph-uganda@ztfministry.org
- **Phone:** +256 785 619613

CPH SOUTH AFRICA

- **Location:** Johannesburg, RSA
- **Email:** tantohtantoh@yahoo.com
- **Phone**: +27 83 744 5682

Made in United States
Orlando, FL
24 March 2025